PREDICTING
RUSSIA'S
FUTURE

BOOKS
BY
RICHARD LOURIE

NONFICTION

RUSSIA SPEAKS: AN ORAL HISTORY FROM THE
REVOLUTION TO THE PRESENT

LETTERS TO THE FUTURE

FICTION

SAGITTARIUS IN WARSAW

FIRST LOYALTY

ZERO GRAVITY

SELECTED TRANSLATIONS

MEMOIRS, BY ANDREI SAKHAROV

THE LIFE AND EXTRAORDINARY ADVENTURES OF
PRIVATE IVAN CHONKIN, BY VLADIMIR VOINOVICH

GOODNIGHT!, BY ANDREI SINYAVSKY

VISIONS FROM SAN FRANCISCO BAY,
BY CZESLAW MILOSZ

MY CENTURY: THE ODYSSEY OF A POLISH
INTELLECTUAL, BY ALEKSANDER WAT

A MINOR APOCALYPSE, BY TADEUSZ KONWICKI

RICHARD LOURIE

WHITTLE DIRECT BOOKS

The Larger Agenda Series is a registered trademark of Whittle Communications L.P.

Time-line photographs, page 1: Nicholas II, Library of Congress; Vladimir Lenin, Brown Brothers; Joseph Stalin, AP/Wide World Photos; Nikita Khrushchev, Brown Brothers; Leonid Brezhnev, TASS for Sovfoto; Mikhail Gorbachev, Sovfoto.
Time-line illustrations, page 1: Genghis Khan, The Bettmann Archive; Ivan the Terrible, Sovfoto; Peter the Great, Library of Congress; Catherine the Great, Library of Congress; Alexander I, Library of Congress; Nicholas I, The Bettmann Archive; Alexander II, Sovfoto.

Illustrations: Russian idol, Sovfoto, page 10; Grand Prince Vladimir, Sovfoto, page 11; Genghis Khan, The Bettmann Archive, page 13; map of the U.S.S.R., by Hayes Cohen, page 17; Mongol invaders, The Bettmann Archive, page 18; Ivan the Terrible, Art Resource, page 33; Peter the Great, Brown Brothers, page 36; Catherine the Great, The Bettmann Archive, page 42; Napoleon's invasion, The Bettmann Archive, page 48; General Mikhail Kutuzov, Sovfoto, page 49; Alexander I, The Bettmann Archive, page 52; Nicholas I, Brown Brothers, page 53; Alexander II, The Bettmann Archive, page 54.

Photographs: Bolshevik Revolution, Brown Brothers, page 63; Nicholas II and family, Brown Brothers, page 64; Leon Trotsky, Sovfoto, page 68; Battle of Stalingrad, Sovfoto, page 70; Nikita Khrushchev, The Bettmann Archive, page 73; Andrei Sakharov, Sipa Press, page 74; Alexander Solzhenitsyn, AP/Wide World Photos, page 81; Mikhail Gorbachev, Patrick Zachmann/Magnum, page 82.

Library of Congress Catalog Number: 91-065098
Lourie, Richard
Predicting Russia's Future
ISBN 0-9624745-9-2
ISSN 1046-364X

The Larger Agenda Series®

The Larger Agenda Series presents original short books by distinguished authors on subjects of importance to managers and policymakers in business and the public sector.

The series is edited and published by Whittle Communications L.P., an independent publishing company. A new book appears approximately every other month. The series reflects a broad spectrum of responsible opinions. In each book the opinions expressed are those of the author, not the publisher or the advertiser.

I welcome your comments on this unique endeavor.

William S. Rukeyser
Editor in Chief

CONTENTS

One Thousand Years of Russian History

988 1000   1100   1240   1300

Grand Prince Vladimir
converts pagan Russia
to Christianity

Mongols invade
and occupy
Kievan Russia

1600   1613

Romanov dynasty
begins

1700   1709   1721   1725

Defeat of Sweden at
Poltava

Peter becomes
first emperor

Peter dies

1801   1812   1825

Alexander I
crowned tsar

Napoleon invades
and is defeated

Alexander I dies;
Nicholas I
crowned tsar

1900   1914   March 1917

World War I begins;
Germany declares war
on Russia

Nicholas II
abdicates

1921   1924   1929   1930-1932

Lenin declares
New Economic
Policy (NEP)

Lenin dies

Trotsky exiled;
Stalin takes
control

Agricultural
collectivizatio

1953

Stalin dies;
Khrushchev elected
general secretary

1979   1982

Invasion of
Afghanistan

Brezhnev dies

1400

1480
Mongol reign ends

1500

1547
Ivan the Terrible
crowned tsar at age 17

1565
Ivan founds the first secret police

1584
Ivan dies

1682
Peter the Great
crowned tsar

1697
Peter tours Europe; first tsar to leave the country

1762
Catherine the Great
seizes the throne

1773
Emelyan Pugachev leads peasant revolt

1796
Catherine dies

1855
Nicholas I dies;
Alexander II crowned tsar

1861
Serfs emancipated

1881
Alexander II assassinated;
Alexander III crowned tsar

1894
Alexander III dies;
Nicholas II crowned tsar

October 1917
Bolshevik Revolution begins

January 1918
Constituent Assembly shut down; Soviet Russian Republic proclaimed

March 1918
Peace treaty signed with Germany

July 1918
Nicholas II and family executed

1920
Lenin's Red Army defeats the White armies

1937-1938
Great Terror and show trials reach peak

1939
Molotov-Ribbentrop Pact signed

1941
Germany invades

1945
Germany defeated

1964
Khrushchev deposed;
Brezhnev elected general secretary

1968
Invasion of Czechoslovakia

1985
Gorbachev elected general secretary

1986
Chernobyl nuclear-reactor accident

1989
Fall of the Berlin Wall

1990
Gorbachev elected president

1991
Military crackdown on Baltic states begins

INTRODUCTION

Thunderclouds have gathered over Russia once again. Will those clouds discharge violent lightning—an armed uprising, a military coup, a civil war?

We shouldn't be surprised that the atmosphere in Russia has turned stormy. A process as momentous as the fall of the House of Communism could not transpire without turmoil and danger. Russia has gone from being stable and stagnant to being awash in possibilities.

The swift changes of democratization frighten the many Russians who see life as a choice between order and anarchy. The lesson they have drawn from their country's long and tragic history is that tyranny is the best guarantee of domestic order and of safety from outside attack. Democracy is simply not a chance worth taking for very long.

But only as a democracy can Russia rejoin the community of civilized nations. Only as a democracy can Russia cease to be a threat to the world. Only as a democracy will Russia survive as more than a third-world economy in the 21st century.

Russia's agony is that it must change but cannot. After engineering the Bolshevik Revolution of 1917, Lenin lived for only six years; it was Stalin who designed and built Soviet Communism. Stalin's system was based on an absolute chain of command that sometimes produced rapid results, but remains unable to absorb change. Even the Soviets finally realized that this system cannot compete in a high-tech world in which information must circulate freely and flexibility is a principal source of strength.

Stalin always got A's in Russian history when he was studying to be a priest in a Georgian seminary. He came to believe that Russians have always preferred the iron order of dictatorship to the confusions of freedom. He once shocked his fellow Communists by saying, "Don't forget we are living in Russia, the land of the tsars. The Russians like to have one man standing at the head of state." Stalin craftily wove the design of his own system into the oldest patterns of the past: the preference for the certainty of tyranny over the vagaries of liberty, the lack of any sense of citizenship, and the popular view that law is an instrument of oppression. Those characteristics run deep in Russia's history and were magnified by the

Soviet experiment. Gorbachev is not only attempting to reform the system that Stalin built; he is also bucking one thousand years of Russian history.

The appeal of Stalin today should not be underestimated. Many Russians are convinced that the current experiment in democracy will fail, and only a strong hand will be able to restore order. The Russians even joke that Soviet history is an alternating series of bald reformers and hairy reactionaries. Bald Lenin was followed by hairy Stalin; bald Khrushchev was followed by hairy Brezhnev; and bald Gorbachev will be followed by . . . ? Whether the next leader will be bald or hairy is of vital importance to us.

After World War II, the United States and the Soviet Union were locked in an arms race, an impasse that seemed as if it would last forever or, still worse, lurch into nuclear holocaust. Then events took a turn—the end of the Cold War—that no one could have foreseen. Yet the "official" end of the Cold War in November 1990 did not mean that we could let Russia slip from mind. In fact, it is more important than ever that we have a clear sense of how Russia operates, for in some ways the destinies of America and Russia are now more tightly linked than ever.

Violent chaos in Russia will impinge on our lives. The use of tactical nuclear weapons in a civil war there could send radiation into our back yards. Waves of Russian refugees would stream west (Sweden and Finland have already constructed camps for refugees fleeing hunger and anarchy), straining the economic and social structure of Europe. Disorder in the U.S.S.R.—food riots, ethnic clashes, terrorism directed against the central government by republics wishing to secede—could lead to the suppression of human rights, a return to totalitarian rule, and a resumption of the arms race. We could lose our newfound alliance with a former enemy and the chance to enforce a new world order, even a *Pax Democratica*.

Thus, it is imperative that American leaders have a realistic picture of the new Russia they want to see emerging from the ruins of the Soviet Union. Merely to project American wishes and ideals will not suffice. The two societies are too different. America is about success, Russia about survival. Happiness and prosperity are beyond most Russians' aspirations; they would gladly settle for a "normal" society, to use a catchword of the early Gorbachev era (by which they mean a society in which enough food reaches the table and people are not jailed for their opinions). But that normal society may not be achieved for some time, and America must prepare for the turbulence that will be the inevitable byproduct of change in a land where change always comes hard.

Economically, a tremendous amount is at stake here. At risk for U.S. business are vast consumer markets. The Russians are potential customers for everything from toothbrushes to personal computers, items we produce well. How would they pay for such products? Though short of hard currency, the Soviet Union possesses vast natural resources—coal, gas, diamonds, timber, gold, and of course oil, of which it remains the world's largest producer. It also has a highly educated work force: one-third of the world's engineers and scientists are in Eastern Europe and the U.S.S.R. As the technology entrepreneur John W. Kiser has noted, those workers are capable of producing "sophisticated results using simple, cheap equipment—an investor's dream." In his recent book *Communist Entrepreneurs*, he cites examples of Soviet technology already sold to the U.S. In biomedicine: intraocular lenses, surgical staples, and ultrasonic surgical scalpels; in metallurgy: techniques for electroslag remelting (metal purification to improve strength), pipe welding, and electromagnetic casting of aluminum. A range of other products and processes have been sold to France, Sweden, and Japan. Russia is a great untapped knowledge base. Though not right now an "investor's dream," Russia has survived worse times, and when the dust settles, the opportunities will be there.

Russia's future is the big guessing game of the late 20th century. But we cannot even attempt to predict its future without a good grounding in its past, if only because the past is still so alive to the Russians today. They will casually mention the Mongol Invasion of 1240 as if it were a relatively recent event, and, as we shall see, it does indeed figure in their furious debate about which road Russia should now take. And though Lenin has been dead for 67 years, the question of whether his revolution was misguided from the start or perverted by Stalin is not in the least academic. The stand that Russians take on these issues will determine their actions in the crucial days to come.

Books about Russia tend to be huge and forbidding like Russia itself. I saw the need for a clear and concise book that would decode Russia's history in order to forecast its future. Such a book would require feats of compression, and obviously many important events and people would have to be omitted. Still, basic patterns of historical behavior could be examined, for it is the essential features of a civilization that recombine in periods of profound change. The goal of the book would be to provide the reader with the rudiments for becoming Russia-literate. I decided to focus on seven key figures

(Prince Vladimir, who converted Russia to Christianity; Ivan the Terrible; Peter the Great; Vladimir Lenin; Joseph Stalin; Andrei Sakharov; and Mikhail Gorbachev) and the three main invasions of Russia (by the Mongols in 1240, Napoleon in 1812, and Hitler in 1941). These struck me as the mandatory minimum.

A news account in the summer of 1990 reinforced my perception that a book of this sort could come in handy. The American advertising firm of Young and Rubicam Sovero opened a Moscow office and, after spending much time and money attempting to do market research, discovered that "unlike Americans, they [the Russians] aren't used to freely giving their opinions, even on the most harmless subject. You have to take a lot of time explaining why you want the information and how it will be used. They are very cagey." What the firm had needed to know was that history has taught the Russians there is no such thing as a "harmless" subject.

I felt especially qualified to write this book after having spent the better part of two years traveling the length and breadth of Russia researching my book *Russia Speaks: An Oral History From the Revolution to the Present*. I spoke with the broadest possible spectrum of Russians—Soviet army colonels, circus clowns, the new businessmen, gravediggers, and icon painters. I traveled from Vilnius in Lithuania to Tashkent near the Chinese border, and from Leningrad in the north to Georgia, Stalin's native land, in the south. No one with whom I spoke had escaped harrowing sorrow, though for many tragedy had only whetted their appetite for life.

Late one winter day in Moscow, after listening to tales of tragedy for 10 hours straight, I was trudging across Red Square when I suddenly broke into a joyful dance. With my arms straight up in the air, I whirled, the ruddy brick of the Kremlin and striped cupolas blurring as I danced in circles. I thanked my grandfather for having the wisdom to leave Russia before the revolution and for his love of liberty, however that taciturn blacksmith may have understood it. Because of him I had not only been born in a free country but had most likely escaped an unenviable fate.

Something in my childhood had stimulated an unflagging curiosity about Russia. Perhaps it was the food I ate in my grandfather's house—black bread, beets, sour cream. Perhaps it was my other Russian-born grandfather's vivid tales of wolves, gypsies, and peasants; or it might have been my father's tight-lipped reluctance to speak of his own youth in Russia. Over the years, that curiosity led me to earn a Ph.D. in Russian studies and resulted in the translation of some 15 books from Russian, including Andrei Sakharov's *Memoirs*. I also wrote three novels and two books of nonfiction, all one way or the other connected with that dark and fascinating land. And now I have produced this book, designed to be a guide to the challenging passage ahead.

It was 1988 when I broke into my dance of lone celebration on Red Square. That year marked the 1,000th anniversary of Christianity in Russia, and the country's dynamic new leader, Mikhail Gorbachev, had allowed that solemn occasion to be celebrated with all due dignity. Church bells tolled again, most of them heavy with the travail of the centuries, some chiming with the promise of redemption. It is the sound of those bells that takes us back to the beginning.

"What a beautiful night for flying."

Louis Turner
Pilot, Seattle

Our planes are equipped with Category III-A avionics, the most advanced in the industry. Which means that our pilots can land in weather when others can't. But more importantly, that we can deliver your shipments on time. When others might be late.

1

CHRISTIAN RUSSIA: GIFT OF THE CROSS

Russia had a happy childhood. The 250 years that followed the country's conversion to Christianity in 988 were the sunniest and most blessed phase of its thousand-year history. The epic suffering that we have come to associate with Russia still lay far in the future and would have seemed as unlikely to the Russians of that time as it now seems inevitable to us.

Christianity has outlasted the various political forms Russia has taken—tsarist, imperialist, Soviet. Today the Church is the primary source of traditional values in a society made cynical by slaughter and deception. But its appeal is more than religious. For many Russians, the Church is the only place where they can connect with their Russian identity.

Very little is known of pagan Russia, whose culture was oral and whose dwellings, temples, and idols were made of wood. There is evidence, however, that the early Russians had an aptitude for agriculture, trade, and warfare. The Arab chronicler Ibn Miskawayh described Russia in the mid-900s as a "mighty nation with . . . great courage. They know not defeat, nor does any of them turn his back till he slay or be slain."

Like most pagans, the early Russians worshiped Mother Earth, but their principal deity was Perun (pronounced "per-*oon*"), god of thunder and lightning. When Perun was impregnating the earth with bolts of lightning during violent storms, the ancient Russians would strip naked and roll in the wet grass with their horses and cattle in the belief that they would all, humans and animals alike, thus acquire some of nature's potent vitality.

Aside from the written observations of a few travelers and other shards of knowledge that have reached us, all that remains of pagan Russia are those myths that lasted long enough to be set down in writing. One such myth tells of the birth of Russia: In the middle of the ninth century, the Vikings were invited to rule the major Russian city of the north, Novgorod. The Russians made this appeal: "Our whole land is great and rich, but there is no order in it. Come to rule and reign over us."

Of course, it is entirely possible that this myth was only a justification for a *fait accompli*—the Vikings might have already invaded and established control, the tale of invitation being invented to save face. In retrospect, the myth seems ominous, for in all the centuries to come, Russia would fail to create a society in which order resulted from the self-governing behavior of citizens. In that regard, the modern Soviet system has failed doubly; neither its individual members nor its innumerable constituent nationalities have any significant loyalty to the idea of larger society.

Even the word *Russia* seems to be Scandinavian in origin and to have come to Novgorod with the Vikings. But history would invest this word with so much meaning that is almost impossible to define today. Russia became the name for both the geographic area radiating for several hundred miles from Moscow and for the tsarist empire that included a hundred nationalities. Now it is also a shorthand way of referring to the Russian Republic, the largest in the U.S.S.R., of which Boris Yeltsin is president. The question of what to call the country confused even Gorbachev in the early days of his administration, when he would frequently say "Russia" when meaning the Soviet Union. That Freudian, or Marxian, slip of the tongue revealed that for Gorbachev the U.S.S.R. had more in common with the old empire of the tsars than he publicly admitted.

The pagan Slavs lived mostly in southern Russia, in what is now the Ukraine. The capital of that region was and still is Kiev, and the grand prince of Kiev was in effect the ruler of the Russians. In 988 Grand Prince Vladimir decided, for reasons both pragmatic and spiritual, that his nation should convert to Christianity. Aware that his people would not surrender their pagan beliefs without struggle, Prince Vladimir acted vigorously, as described in *The Tale of Bygone Years*, a chronicle kept by churchmen: " . . . he directed that the idols should be overthrown and that some should be cut to pieces and others burned with fire. He thus ordered that Perun should be bound to a horse's tail and dragged . . . to the river. He appointed twelve men to beat the idols with sticks."

This was the first instance of what would become a quintessential Russian act: that of tearing down the images of one god and raising up those of another. Perun, Christ, Stalin—shifts in power have usually been preceded or signaled by shifts in the worship of sacred idols and icons. Until Lenin's tomb, the very symbol of the revolution, is removed from Red Square, the Soviet Russians will not have made a leap as dramatic as Vladimir's.

Vladimir accepted Christianity from the Greek Orthodox empire of Byzantium, not Rome. No split had yet occurred between the two great branches of the church—the Latin West and the Greek East—and Russia was closer to Byzantium, with which it both warred and traded. Only much later would it become apparent what a fateful choice Vladimir had made, one in part responsible for cutting Russia off from the dynamics of Western Christendom. Other consequences of his choice were felt more immediately. The translation used in the Russian church service was close enough to the Slavic vernacular to make the study of Greek and the other classical languages unnecessary for either clergy or laymen. There was also a millenarian doctrine widely accepted at the time that predicted the world would end in the year 1000. Thus the Church did not stress the analysis of biblical texts but rather the "proper praise" of God, the literal meaning of the word *orthodoxy*.

The Christianity introduced in Russia was a religion of forgiveness, but not of tolerance, at least not of other religions. Orthodox Christianity taught Russia that it held the "one truth," for truth, like God, could only be one. The Renaissance of Western Europe gradually eroded a similar doctrine of the Roman Catholic Church, but nothing of the sort ever took place in Russia. In what other country could the official ruling party's newspaper be called *Pravda* ("The Truth") without people falling down laughing?

Pagan Russians commonly worshiped household gods such as the wooden idol above, which was excavated from the city of Novgorod.

Prince Vladimir not only found his subjects reluctant to give up their pagan gods, he found them adamant in their attachment to alcohol. The following couplet is attributed to the grand prince himself: "The Russian cannot bear to think/Of life devoid of all strong drink."

When Gorbachev came to power in 1985, one of his first attempts at reform was his antidrinking campaign, which quickly failed. Sugar disappeared from the stores as moonshiners worked overtime. Because the alcohol industry is state-owned, government revenues plunged. The campaign was called off, the reformer defeated by a problem with roots running a thousand years deep.

No doubt Vladimir hoped that the introduction of Christianity would inspire his subjects to create a stronger society. It may, however, have had the opposite effect. Christianity makes a strong distinction between the world and the soul, between Caesar and God. The Russians may have used that distinction as a justification for neglecting the prosaic tasks that build social order.

Drinking to excess has not been confined to the suffering masses.

Grand Prince Vladimir is shown here converting the people of Kiev to Christianity in 988, marking the end of pagan Russia.

Peter the Great was an epic imbiber, Stalin's entourage has been described as constantly half-sloshed, and Boris Yeltsin has been in trouble more than once for his alleged propensity for strong drink. The way alcoholism is dealt with could have great influence on a society that is facing the imperative of dealing seriously with the sober issues of stability and prosperity. If the Russians can shake their thousand-year addiction to alcohol, they may be capable of transforming their society.

The political history of Kievan Russia is filled with civil war caused largely by an imperfect system of princely successions whose complexities led inevitably to disputes and clashes. It has been estimated, for example, that the country suffered civil war in at least 80 of the 170 years between 1054 and 1224.

The glories of Kiev far outshone its shortcomings, however; Russia had made a "brilliant debut," as one historian put it. And another, Serge Zenkovsky, in his introduction to *Medieval Russia's Epics, Chronicles, and Tales*, described its grandeur:

> Kiev itself became one of the wealthiest and most animated cities of medieval Europe, richer and more brilliant than Paris or London of the time. It was adorned with innumerable churches, and by the time

of the reign of Vladimir's son, Yaroslav, . . . there were already numerous schools, hospitals, libraries. In the eleventh and twelfth centuries Russia was an integral part of Europe, and Kievan princes maintained close dynastic ties with the ruling houses of Western countries. . . . A daughter of Prince Yaroslav, Anna, married King Phillip of France and was the only literate member of the French royal family for whom she signed state documents herself.

Unlike the rest of medieval Europe, which used the barter system, Kievan Russia's economy was based on money. Favorably situated on the great north-to-south trade route between Scandinavia and Byzantium (now part of Turkey), Russia flourished in both foreign trade and domestic commerce. (One cannot, however, note without a certain melancholy that one aspect of the situation of a thousand years ago hasn't changed: the country remains an exporter of raw materials rather than finished products.)

Architecture and literature thrived. The early Russian religious tales are like crude yet charming folk carvings; by the middle of the 12th century, Russia had its first masterpiece, an epic poem called "The Song of Igor's Campaign," which has been translated into English by Vladimir Nabokov. Like a faded fresco in a 12th-century cathedral, the poem still retains its original vigor and color. A prince dreams:

> They ladled out for me
> A blue wine mixed with sorrow

The poem goes on to foreshadow internal strife and civil war:

> And brother said to brother:
> 'This is mine,
> and that also is mine.'
> And the princes began to argue about trifles
> calling them important matters
> and began to create discord among themselves.

Still, the fall of Kievan Russia would not be caused by internal discord alone, but by an external force: the Mongol Invasion of 1240. George Vernadsky, the leading expert on the period, characterizes Russia in its historical childhood as a country of "free political institutions and free interplay of social and economic forces." Unfortunately that was not to be Kievan Russia's legacy to subsequent generations, for whom such freedoms would seem at best a distant memory, a dangerous luxury. The invasion of the Mongols and their 250-year domination caused Russia to take an entirely different path, one that emphasized the safety of tyranny over the vulnerabilities of freedom. When, in late December 1990, the head of the KGB warned of poisoned wheat from the West, he was not only playing on the fears instilled by Soviet propaganda, but on the bitter historical truth Russians learned from the Mongol Invasion and those of Napoleon and Hitler: Danger comes from without.

Christianity was Kievan Russia's gift and legacy to posterity, the one golden strand of continuity that runs throughout Russian history and still shines brightly today. Large numbers of young people are now turning to the Orthodox Church again—for a sense of Russian identity, for solace in a collapsing society, for the beauty of its service, art, and architecture amid the stained gray concrete of socialism.

But the Church's saving graces contain dangers as well. When collecting material for my oral history of Russia, I decided to seek out an interview with a priest. I asked a married couple I knew—intellectuals in their early thirties who had embraced Russian orthodoxy with a fervor that did not preclude either humor or tolerance—if they would arrange a meeting for me with their priest, of whom they always spoke with passionate admiration. They agreed. But they were downcast when they returned from Sunday mass.

"Did you ask him?" I said.

"We did."

"And what did he say?"

"No."

"Why?"

"He says there are only two books in the world, the Bible and Solzhenitsyn's *The Gulag Archipelago*, and no need for any others."

The exchange reveals the seeds of a Russian fundamentalism that, given the right conditions of chaos and crisis, could combine with nationalism to produce a strange new social order ruled by priests and generals.

By the middle of the 13th century, Kiev had grown weaker. Civil strife played a part, as did a change in trade routes that reduced the city's commercial importance. Yet those were negligible factors compared with the coming of Genghis Khan and the Golden Horde, as his armies were later known. A Novgorodian chronicle

In addition to invading Kievan Russia in 1224, Genghis Khan (1162-1227) captured Peking, Iran, and Iraq during his expansion of the Mongolian empire.

notes for the year 1224 that "in that same year, for our sins,, there came unknown tribes." The Russians were used to defending themselves against nomadic tribes that swept in from the east and south, winning some battles, losing others. But this enemy was different. The Mongols and their Tartar shock troops were not content with victorious battle and the spoils thereof. In a portent of the grandiose cruelty soon to come, the captured Russian princes were, as the Novgorodian chronicle notes, "taken by the Tartars and crushed beneath platforms placed over their bodies on the top of which the Tartars celebrated their victory banquet." Then the new invaders disappeared as suddenly as they had arrived. "We know neither from whence they came nor whither they have now gone."

They had withdrawn to Mongolia because Genghis Khan had died in 1227. But the transition of power was orderly in the horde, and why the Mongols did not quickly reappear is something of a mystery. Russia was obviously not yet a priority for them.

The Mongols were not heard from for another 13 years. Then they returned by the tens of thousands, and Russia's childhood—sunlit, tumultuous, princely—came to an abrupt and bloody end. It would never again be the same.

THE MONGOLS: A BITTER WISDOM

"**S**cratch a Russian and you'll find a Tartar," quipped Napoleon. Probably all he meant was that the Russians, for all their European trappings—their palaces, wigs, footmen, and command of French—were essentially Asiatic barbarians. He was not to remain alone in that opinion. Alexander Blok, an early-20th-century Russian poet, reminded the West that "Yes, we are Asiatics./With slanting and greedy eyes." And Stalin once confided to the ambassador from Japan: "We are Asiatics too."

The question of whether Russia belongs to the West or the East, or neither, has been debated in Russia for centuries. The Mongol Invasion is one source of the current struggle over which direction Russia should take. The argument has produced two schools of thought. The Westernizers assert that the Russians would do best by emulating the European model of democracy, tolerance, and rule of law. The Slavophiles insist that Russia has a nature, a history, and a destiny of its own that are neither European nor Asiatic.

The origin of the question lies in 1240, when the Mongols returned to Russia, where they would remain for approximately 250 years. An event that took place that long ago might seem of little contemporary relevance, but to the Russians the significance of that invasion remains both a subject of heated debate and a starting point for discussion about the country's future.

In the fall of 1990, the exiled novelist Alexander Solzhenitsyn published a 16,000-word essay, "How to Revitalize Russia," calling for the orderly dissolution of the Soviet Union and the formation of an "all-Slav state" to be composed of Russia, Belorussia, and the Ukraine. The key element was the Ukraine, rich in farmland, coal, and energy. But what if the Ukraine was not interested in such an arrangement? That, according to Solzhenitsyn, would be at best a misunderstanding, for all three nationalities were originally one people "separated into three branches by the terrible tragedy of the Mongol Invasion. . . . We all issue from the precious city of Kiev, 'from which the Russian land takes its origin,' as *The Tale of Bygone Years* says, and from which we received the light of Christianity." In Russia the distinction between ancient history and current events is at best tenuous.

The 1240 Mongol Invasion was led by Batu Khan, a grandson of Genghis. Batu had an army of some 200,000 highly mobile cavalry, which, as the historian Nicholas Riasanovsky describes, moved "with great speed on frozen rivers—the only successful winter invasion of Russia in history." In addition to horsemen, the horde had experts in siege warfare, and no city on earth could withstand its onslaught—least of all the Russian cities of that day, which were weakened by internal strife and failing commerce. But neither unity nor wealth could have provided sufficient defense against the murderous skill and sheer numbers of the horde.

Kiev was put to the torch, its citizens exterminated. The history of the period, recorded by churchmen and monks, describes all the Russian cities through which the horde had passed as nothing but "smoke, ashes, and barren earth. . . . And not one man remained alive in the city. All were dead. All had drunk the same bitter cup to the dregs. And there was not even anyone to mourn the dead. Neither father nor mother could mourn their dead children, nor the children their father and mother. . . . All of this happened according to the will of God because of our sins."

Like Perun, Russia's new Christian God could suddenly hurl lightning bolts at sinful Russia. The churchmen created a version of events in which the Christian God remained omnipotent, if dark and harsh.

The Russians fled north in large numbers. They may have believed that the Mongols were instruments of God's punishment, but the Russians proved adept at being grandly philosophical and brutally realistic at the same time. The shift of population changed the geopolitical shape of Russia. The next great Russian capital emerged in Moscow, at that time only a meager settlement on a muddy river.

The Russians had been slaughtered and enslaved by the Mongols. Now they followed the rule of the khan. Though Russian princes were allowed to rule their own principalities and even to make war, they had to travel to the khan and make obeisance to him. No important decisions could be made without his permission.

Unlike the Romans, for example, the Mongols were not in the

Russia (after Mongol occupation)

The exiled novelist Alexander Solzhenitsyn called for the formation of an all-Slavic union composed of the Russian, Belorussian, and Ukrainian republics. The name *Russia* refers specifically to the Russian Republic, one of 15 republics that compose the U.S.S.R. Russia includes Siberia and stretches from Leningrad and Moscow in the west to the Pacific Ocean in the east.

***The Conquerors*, by Novgorodian painter V. V. Vereshchagin (1842-1904), depicts a scene from the Mongol Invasion of 1240, which led to the slaughter of most of the citizens of Kiev.**

least interested in imposing their culture on the people they had conquered. Supreme realists, the Mongols were interested only in money and power. The money accrued to them from severe taxes that were collected for them by the Russian princes, and the Mongols' power was enforced by devastating punitive raids if those princes withheld money or rose in revolt. Otherwise, the Mongols were content to rule from afar.

For that reason, few traces of the Mongols' occupation were left behind. Linguists, for example, have been unable to find many derivations from the Mongol language, with the significant exception of the Russian word for money: *dengi*. The historian Charles Halperin described one of the few other influences in *Russia and the Golden Horde*: ". . . Sixteenth-century descriptions of the typical Muscovite cavalryman show him in a Mongol saddle with Mongol stirrups, wearing a Mongol helmet, and armed with a Mongol compound bow with a Mongol quiver."

One of the odder legacies of the Mongol, or Tartar, domination is culinary. Nomadic horsemen, the Tartars favored a meal of raw beef mixed with onions and spices. That dish seems to have migrated west through Novgorod to Germany. The Tartar's favorite dish became known as beef tartare and is still standard fare in the better European restaurants. Apparently it became quite popular in the city of Hamburg, where the locals decided the meat would taste better cooked, thus creating a variant that came to be known as the hamburger. Thus, when the first McDonald's was opened in Moscow, it was a homecoming, in a certain sense—the closing of an old circle.

The Russians' costs from the Mongol Invasion were great; they lost much of their population, cities, and libraries, in addition to their independence and the dignity of freedom. Moreover, they were isolated from Europe and the first stirrings of the Renaissance. In the years between the baptism of Russia in 988 and the arrival of the Mongols in 1240, Russia had been closely aligned with the great dynasties of Europe. By the time Russia was free of the Mongols, the new Europe was exploring not only the open seas, but a world of new ideas. Russia was just regaining its independence when Leonardo da Vinci was sketching rudimentary designs for helicopters and Christopher Columbus was setting sail westward in search of a new route to India.

The Mongols were quirky conquerors. They did not interfere in local politics, even allowing the democratic institution of town meetings to continue. They also did much to stimulate the spiritual and economic power of the Russian Orthodox Church. Halperin remarks that tolerance for all religions was part of the Golden Horde's tradition: "The Mongols required of the Church only that it pray for the health of the khan. . . . The immense tax privileges the khans granted the Church enabled it to recover from the losses suffered during the invasion . . . and prosper as never before."

The impact of the Mongol occupation was not only profound but paradoxical. Devastating the land, slaughtering the population, the Mongols at the same time strengthened the one force that could

"I can make a BMW go faster."

Friedrich Winther
Freight Handler, Dingolfing, W. Germany

By using Federal Express® to fly BMW parts to the U.S. directly from Germany, BMW
dealers can make customers' cars fly out of the shop in just days.

keep the Russian identity alive. Christianity now proved more valuable than Prince Vladimir could have ever foreseen. The soul of Russia had been saved by religion and a tax break.

The time of the Mongol occupation is traditionally referred to as the Tartar, or Mongol Yoke, period, invoking images of humiliation, servitude, and reduction to the level of beasts of burden. That description held for all areas of life, except for the Church, which was not only a link to the past but a refuge from the present. Though everything else went into precipitous decline—industry, literature, the crafts, education—the Church enjoyed a renaissance of its own, especially in the art of icon painting.

The icon had come to Russia along with Christianity from Byzantium and would achieve its greatest prominence there. An icon is not merely a work of art but an instrument of spirituality, like prayer, and serves as a window onto heaven. Before setting to work, an icon painter would fast, pray, and make confession. The icons Russia produced during the period of the Mongol domination are one of the glories of Russian culture; those fashioned by Andrei Rublev (1370-1430) are among the world's masterpieces of religious art.

The word *icon* can also connote any especially sacred symbol, and Russian history has been a war of symbols since the day Vladimir ordered the statues of Perun, God of Thunder, "cut to pieces . . . bound to a horse's tail . . . and dragged to the river." The Soviets, like Vladimir, could not tolerate the existence of any other faith. Priests were killed, icons smashed, churches turned into clubs or warehouses. Lenin was mummified and deified. On Stalin's 70th birthday in 1949, a gigantic image of the Great Leader was projected onto the clouds in the night sky over Moscow. When Stalin died in 1953, his body was embalmed and placed beside Lenin's (it was later to be slipped out of the mausoleum by night as part of Khrushchev's anti-Stalinist campaign). The domestic battle of symbols continues. According to a Reuters wire-service dispatch in November 1990, Gorbachev has "ordered a stop to the removal of monuments honoring Lenin. . . . Mr. Gorbachev issued a decree . . . ordering the security forces to take additional measures to protect monuments to Lenin, the civil war, World War II, and the workers' movement."

This was done partly to placate conservatives, but shrewd leader that he is, Gorbachev also knows that it is still too early to remove the traditional Soviet icons, which at least symbolize familiar values. When will Russia have new icons, and what will they be? Can we expect to see statues of Sakharov, Solzhenitsyn, or Gorbachev springing up all over Russia, from Red Square to the humblest township whose little park always has its bust of Lenin or Marx gazing down on the children playing and the drunks sleeping it off on the benches? Which icons are cast down and which are raised up will be one sure indicator of which way the wind is blowing in Russia. Assuming that the Russians retain their predilection for sacred images, the best that one could hope for is a pluralistic iconography, that is, tolerance manifested by a variety of symbols.

I keep a mental checklist of Soviet icons, and I note that at the beginning of 1991 Lenin was still in his tomb, the bust of Stalin immediately to the left of the mausoleum remained in place, and the statue of Felix Dzerzhinsky, the founder of the Soviet secret police, still towered on its pedestal in front of KGB headquarters in the heart of Moscow. And Communism's ruby-red stars still glow on the Kremlin's towers. The old symbols are still in place.

Kremlin is simply the Russian word for "fortress," and every old Russian city had one. Had history taken a slightly different course, we might be referring to "the Kremlin" in Novgorod or Pskov, cities that at the time of the Mongol Invasion were much more developed than Moscow. The princes of Moscow served the Mongols faithfully by refusing to join rebellions against them and by always delivering their taxes on time. Moscow's population increased with refugees from cities that had risen against the Mongols, who had then retaliated with raids.

Moscow also gradually became the seat of the Russian Church in 1328, thus fostering an identification of city, Church, and nation. Patriotism and Moscow became roughly synonymous. The Mongol strategy had been to conquer then divide to prevent any serious opposition from developing. Feigning slavish allegiance to the khan, Moscow quietly increased its own size and power. By the time the leaders of the Golden Horde realized how strong Moscow had become, it was too late. Their empire had been weakened by plague and attacked by Asiatic rivals, and now Moscow's spears were able to gradually push the horde back in the direction from which it had come thundering 250 years before. No single decisive battle lives in Russian history as the moment when the Mongol yoke was finally thrown off. A Russian army defeated the Mongols for the first time at the Battle of Kulikovo Field in 1380, a psychologically bracing, yet isolated encounter. The Mongols would remain Russia's rulers for another 100 years.

The 250-year occupation was time enough for the Russians to

learn a bitter and essential lesson. If they were not to fall victim again, they must imitate and even exceed the might of their vanquisher. They had seen that the Mongols' superiority lay not only in warfare, but in their ability to administer the lands they had conquered. As the historian Charles Halperin says, the Mongols' postal system was the "fastest communications system across the Eurasian continent that had ever been known." But more important than any single attribute was the very shape of the Mongol state—a monolithic pyramid ruled by the khan to whom the Russians referred as tsar, a title with connotations of omnipotence that no Russian ruler had ever assumed.

The Russians internalized the Mongol system, which would form and deform all their future political and social development. In his definitive book *Kievan Russia*, Yale professor of Russian history George Vernadsky described the reasons for the new power structure:

> . . . a glance at the political history of Russia is sufficient to dispose of the myth of totalitarianism's being inherent in the Russian mentality. It was not because of any alleged innate sympathy of the 'Russian soul' to autocracy that the tsardom of Moscow came into being but out of the stern necessity of organizing a military force sufficient to overthrow the Mongol yoke and then of securing control of a territory vast enough for strategic defense. Muscovy became a military camp. The energy of both rulers and people was concentrated on defense.

Vernadsky's conclusion touches the painful essence of Russia's history: "Political freedom was sacrificed for national survival."

Such was Russia's fateful choice, not a conscious decision but a silent understanding. Spiritually, Russia had interpreted the Mongol domination as a punishment for its sins. But once free of the Mongols, Russia became realistic, building ramparts, forging spears, and collecting taxes. Now the country's task was to reunite its severed parts and build a state that was a fortress. Soon enough, that state would have a mighty leader of its own, its first tsar, Ivan IV: Ivan the Terrible.

3

IVAN THE TERRIBLE: THE MADNESS OF A GENIUS

The arrival in 1564 of a letter from Prince Kurbsky, a former trusted general who had joined with Poland, Russia's enemy, so infuriated Ivan that he drove the iron point of his staff through the messenger's foot, nailing it to the floor. Ivan made the poor man stand there while a servant read the letter aloud. Unfortunately for that bearer of bad news, those were not days when brevity was considered the soul of wit.

Ivan's spontaneous act of cruelty accords with his notorious reputation. But his ensuing 15-year correspondence with the defector reveals unsuspected complexities of character and mind. That Ivan took time out from the demands of rebuilding a country left in pieces by the Mongols to correspond with Kurbsky is surprising. Even more surprising is that his letters were written well enough to make them an essential part of every anthology of old Russian literature. Ivan's major impact, of course, was far from literary. He was the architect of Russian totalitarianism, and his influence on the Russian state remains to this day. In his fearful and lonely youth, however, Ivan had devoted considerable time to reading and was later considered one of the most erudite men in Russia, even by those who loathed him.

The sacred image, the icon, had by that time become an integral part of Russian culture, and now it was matched by a belief in the incantatory power of words. At times a deeply, pathologically fervent Christian, Ivan believed that "in the beginning was the Word," and because God had appointed him to begin Russia anew, Ivan too must of necessity be a master of the word. Ivan not only understood the spiritual power of words, he realized their relationship to political power.

The idea of becoming Russia's first tsar was Ivan's; he proposed it to the wealthy aristocrats, known as boyars, who competed, often successfully, for power with the grand princes. The boyars were surprised by Ivan's request, but they were essentially indifferent. Grand prince, tsar—what's in a name? But Ivan, though only 17 at the time, knew from extensive reading that the word *tsar* had been emblazoned on the Russian mind; in the Russian translation of the Bible, the ancient kings of Israel were always called tsar. *Tsar* was also the usual term used in referring to the emperors of Rome and Byzantium, not to mention the khans of the Golden Horde. Ivan's dream was to possess absolute authority. In the beginning was the word, and the word was *tsar*.

By assuming this title, Ivan had by association made himself the legitimate heir to the two centers of Christianity, Rome and Byzantium. His new position corresponded with a widespread belief that had gained currency in Moscow at that time, which held that the city was the Third Rome, and the last. Ivan now had a Messianic vision that could justify any crime he committed. And Ivan's dream of a reunited Russia would require many crimes.

Ivan believed he had a singular relationship with God. The French biographer Henri Troyat, in his magisterial life of Ivan, depicts this relationship: "The Almighty was temperamental: One day He overlooked everything, the next He hurled thunderbolts because of a peccadillo. Unpredictable and disordered, He had, in fact, the same character as Ivan. God was another Ivan, a super-Ivan." To challenge the tsar was both treason and blasphemy. Many of his letters ended with the following salutation: "We, humble Ivan, Tsar and Grand Prince of all the Russians by the grace of God, and not by the restless will of men."

Russia had made its fateful choice between survival and liberty, and Ivan was the first full-blown expression of what that choice would mean in practice: the greater the cruelty the state could inflict on its own people, the greater the cruelty it could inflict on an enemy.

The Mongols had kept Russia divided into a multitude of principalities, both for administrative purposes and to prevent the emergence of any center of power to challenge their authority. There could be no truly strong Russia until all those various bits and pieces had been welded into a mighty fortress of state. The reforging of Russia, a process known as the "gathering of the Russian lands," was already under way by the time of Ivan's birth in 1530. He inherited from the grand princes of the past the quest for reunification; he would accelerate and largely complete the process by reacquiring lands during the years of his reign.

Ivan, who was orphaned early, might never have ascended the throne, for which he became eligible at age 3. The contentious boyars fought among themselves for political dominance and would have murdered Ivan if they hadn't considered him a mere child of no threat to them. Throughout his life Ivan complained of abuse at the hands of the boyars, justifying his cruelties not only as his God-given right but as just vengeance for what he deemed the humiliations of his youth. His regal sensitivity to the merest slight was exquisite. In one letter, Ivan wrote, "Me and my brother Yuri, of blessed memory, they brought up like vagrants and children of the poorest. What I have not suffered for want of garments and food! . . . I shall mention just one thing: once in my childhood we were playing, and Prince Ivan Vasilevich Shuisky was sitting on a bench, leaning with his elbow against our father's bed, and even putting his foot upon it."

Ivan bided his time, reading deeply and mastering the science of sadism. Troyat writes: "He would tear the feathers from birds he caught, put out their eyes, slit their stomachs with a knife, delight in watching the stages by which they died. Standing on the ramparts of the Kremlin fortress, he would whirl young dogs above his head and hurl them down to the courtyard to break their bones. Their plaintive yelps satisfied an obscure need for revenge, as if these were the hateful boyars he was putting to death."

He would have his revenge over the boyars soon enough. Five years after being crowned tsar in 1547, Ivan, age 22, firmly ensconced himself by conquering the Tartar capital of Kazan. His proclivities for cruelty and vengeance, though, were restrained by two forces: what he considered to be the hand of God, and the influence of his virtuous wife, Anastasia, whom he respected and adored. But nothing could keep his pathological side entirely in check. To commemorate the victory of Kazan, Ivan ordered a great cathedral built on Red Square. Known now as the Cathedral of Basil the Blessed, its fanciful, multicolored cupolas have made it synonymous with Russia and the favorite backdrop for correspondents reporting live from Moscow. Legend has it that Ivan was so taken with the beauty of the cathedral that upon its completion he at once ordered the architect blinded so he could never create anything so grand anywhere else.

Ivan's subjects accepted his severity. The English author Giles Fletcher noted in *Of the Russe Common Wealth*, published in 1591: "A great people, inert and silent, regarding with a mixture of love and terror this father of the great Russian family, this living law, this representative of God on earth, whose very crimes were accepted as a punishment sent by God to his people and to whose cruelty they must submit, for it created martyrs and opened the doors of heaven."

Ivan's psychopathic cruelty was fully unleashed only after the death of Anastasia in 1560. Joseph Stalin's words upon the death of his first wife could well have been spoken by Ivan: "This creature used to soften my stony heart. When she died, all my warm feelings for people died with her." Like Stalin, Ivan was able to align his psychoses with his policies. Suspecting that Anastasia had been poisoned by the boyars, the very enemies he wished to eradicate, he let loose a wave of terror on Russia. "A man no longer dared to speak freely among his friends, was careful what he said within his family, and kept silent at public gatherings, with fear in the pit of the stomach."

That this description by Troyat holds true for both Ivan's Russia of the mid-16th century and Stalin's of the mid-20th century is not a coincidence. To a large extent, Stalin modeled himself on Ivan; he was responsible for the official Soviet view of Ivan as a progressive tsar who, by increasing the size of the country and repressing the conservative boyars, impelled Russia along the road to revolution and Communism. When the great Russian film director Sergey Eisenstein was creating his two-part film on the life of Ivan the Terrible, Stalin took a more than casual interest in how Ivan would be depicted, for he knew that the always allegorical-minded Russians would see him in Ivan.

It would be logical to assume that tyrants such as Ivan and Stalin are loathed by their people. But human nature, especially in Russia, is more complicated than that. A shrewd observer of Ivan captured the essence of the Russian reaction to him: " . . . I think no prince in Christendom is more feared of his own than he is, nor yet better beloved." Both men had lent grandeur to Russia by increasing its size and power, and also by their legendary cruelty. Both men were only keeping the bargain Russia had made with itself.

Ivan created the first Russian secret police. In *KGB: The Inside Story*, the British historian Christopher Andrew and former KGB colonel Oleg Gordievsky note that "Russia's first political police was founded in 1565 by Ivan the Terrible. . . . The six thousand [secret police] dressed in black, rode on black horses, and carried on their saddles the emblems of a dog's head and a broom, symbolizing their mission to sniff out and sweep away treason."

Ivan's furies knew no bounds. His enemies—anyone he suspected of treason or harboring ill intent—were tortured until they confessed to the crimes of which they were accused. Terror served his dual policy of exterminating internal opponents of his absolute rule and of further unifying the Russian lands. His wrath fell on individuals, families, even entire cities. Novgorod, that city-state that had once sent princes packing and had preserved its democratic town meeting, proved particularly reluctant to accept Ivan's vision. But Ivan knew the cure for obstinacy. During a five-week period in 1570, nearly all of that city's inhabitants were massacred. But massacre was the least of it. By this time Ivan and his eldest son (and namesake) had grown very close, for they shared a love of learning and a fascination with torture. Father and son were together during the martyrdom of Novgorod, which Troyat describes as follows:

> Every day in the great square a thousand inhabitants were brought before him [Ivan] and his son—notables, merchants, or ordinary citizens. No interrogation, no hearing of witnesses, no pleading, no verdict. Simply by virtue of the fact that these people lived in Novgorod, the accursed city, they were guilty. To further perfect the punishment, husbands were tortured in front of wives, mothers in front of children. The [secret police] flogged their victims with knouts, broke their limbs, cut out their tongues, slit their nostrils, castrated them, roasted them over slow fires. Then, bleeding and broken, the poor wretches were tied by the head or feet to sleighs, which sped over the snow toward . . . a place where even in the depths of winter the river remained open. There they were flung into the icy water, whole families at a time, wives with their husbands, mothers with babies at their breasts. Those who rose to the surface were dispatched with boat hooks, lances, and axes by [secret police] in boats. The methodical slaughter lasted for five weeks. Ivan and his son never tired of the spectacle.

It was not simply that father and son took the sadist's delight in inflicting and observing pain. They were both intellectually fascinated by the revelations about human psychology that only torture affords. Exactly how long does dignity endure? Exactly how many minutes can courage last?

In 1571, the year after the martyrdom of Novgorod, the Tartars suddenly swept in from the steppes and burned Moscow to the ground, though they were unable to take the Kremlin. Ivan began

"Thanks to me,
Air-Vet's business is going to the dogs."

Cheryl Kelley
Business Logistics Account Representative, Philadelphia

And the cats, horses, pigs and sheep. Because for Air-Vet, a leading veterinary supply company, turning over its warehousing and distribution to our Business Logistics Services division was the right prescription for building business. So now, not only can vets' orders be filled overnight, but in the fiercely competitive veterinary supply industry, Air-Vet is on its way to becoming top dog.

to suffer reverses in the Baltic states, where he had earlier won brilliant victories against the ruling German knights, who stood between Russia and the Baltic Sea. (Today's problems in the Baltic states go back 500 years and are based on the same motive: access to the sea.) Perhaps fearing that "my own Tsar Jesus Christ" had turned against him, Ivan now abolished his secret police; in a dramatic reversal of policy, he decreed that anyone who so much as mentioned them was to be whipped with a knout in a public square. The historian Bernard Pares once wrote of Ivan that "the new system which he set up was madness, but the madness of a genius." But this mad genius had also been favored by fortune. Hardy Muscovite explorers, backed up by Cossacks, claimed Siberia's vast, rich lands for Ivan, turning Russia into the giant it has been ever since. This expansion is reminiscent of America's drive west, and for once the Russians got a head start: they reached the Pacific in 1649, just 29 years after the Pilgrims landed at Plymouth. Russian explorers, traders, and hunters ventured into Alaska, which Russia owned until 1867, when the U.S. bought it for the bargain price of $7,200,000 (think how much worse the Cold War would have been had Alaska remained in Russian hands).

Though necessity and opportunity kept Ivan's gaze fixed eastward, he became increasingly aware of the West after the chance landing of an English ship in northern Russia—an event that led to commercial relations with England. Trade had made Ivan aware of the great world that lay to the west of his kingdom. At one point he even took it into his head to join the East and West by offering his hand in marriage to Queen Elizabeth. An odder couple could hardly be imagined; the queen found a way of politely refusing his proposal.

Though retaining a sense of Russian superiority and a belief in Moscow as the Third Rome, Ivan was nonetheless impressed by the West's progress in technology, armaments, and medicine. For their part, Westerners coming to Muscovy felt they had entered a forbidding kingdom where everyone ruled by the whip. *The Household Manager*, a book that codified all aspects of Russian daily life, suggests the culture they encountered there. It advised the following for the rearing of sons: "If you love your son, beat him frequently; in the end he will be a joy to you. . . . Do not laugh with him, do not play with him, for if you weaken in small things you will suffer in great ones. . . . Break his heart while he is growing up, for if it hardens, he will not obey you." It issued quite specific instructions for the beating of wives as well. Blows to the head and heart were to

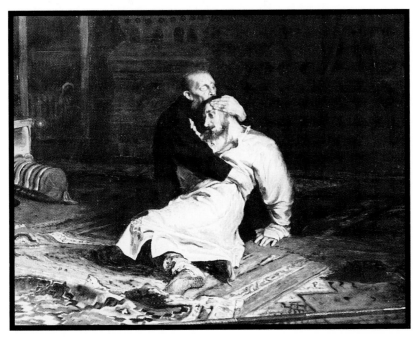

This painting by Ilya Repin (1844-1930) portrays Ivan the Terrible's horror upon realizing he had mortally wounded his son, whom he suspected of plotting against him.

be avoided, and the whip was preferred over blunt instruments. Before beating her, a husband should remove his wife's blouse so as not to ruin a perfectly good article of clothing. Upon completion, endearments should be whispered to her. If God was a super-Ivan, then the father of a Russian family was a miniature tsar.

Over time, Ivan's paranoia grew and spread. The only person it seemed to spare was his son Ivan, who continued to indulge his father's passions for scholarship and sadism. When not attending court ceremonies or accompanying his father to the torture chambers, the young Ivan was writing a biography of St. Anthony. But suspicion proved even greater than a father's love. Convinced that his own son was plotting against him, Ivan struck him in a fit of rage with his sharp iron-tipped staff, a second later realizing to his horror that he had inflicted a mortal wound upon his beloved son. For four days the young Ivan hovered between life and death. He recovered consciousness once, and he kissed his father's hands, saying, "I die as your devoted son and the most submissive of your subjects."

Ivan was demented with grief. He drew up long lists of all his past victims on sheets of parchment and sent them to monasteries with money to pay for prayers to be said for their souls. But Ivan could not sleep, and his health began to fail. Troyat imagines how Ivan might have rationalized the murder of his son: "God too was accountable for the blood of His child, the Christ. He had let Jesus perish on the cross. Both of them had murdered their sons. God and the Tsar were two of a kind."

Ivan himself died in 1584, three years after killing his son. A Soviet autopsy revealed that the 54-year-old tsar had been poisoned, though it was never ascertained by whose hand.

Ivan left a Russia mighty and united, though still barbarous in its ignorance. Before Ivan was even born, Europe had already seen the genius of da Vinci, the Sistine Chapel, and Martin Luther's reforms. But Russia had experienced its own renaissance. One hundred years after the end of the Mongol domination, Russia had been reborn.

PETER THE GREAT: LIGHT FROM THE WEST

P eter was a giant, nearly seven feet tall. His stride and pace were so great that his retinue of ministers and advisers was forever panting to keep up with him. His boots, large enough for a boy to hide in, still inspire awe from their display case in the Kremlin Museum. Peter the Great fully deserved his name, not only because of his height, but because of the grandeur of his ambitions and achievements. Though he consumed food, liquor, and women with gargantuan gusto, he thirsted for nothing so much as knowledge from the West.

When Gorbachev came to power, he was frequently compared to Peter. Both men tried to impose Western ways on Russia. But the Russians never quite trusted the West enough to embrace ideas that challenged their enduring preference for order over liberty.

The first tsar ever to leave Russia, Peter made his initial trip to Western Europe in 1697, when he was 25 years old. He charmed European royalty with his curiosity and intelligence and horrified them with his manners, belching and farting at the table. He caroused on a scale that matched the vastness of his land, but he was still up every day before dawn acquiring the utilitarian knowledge of the West. He studied everything, including dentistry. God help the Russian who complained of a toothache in Peter's presence; in a trice the tsar would have his instruments out and in the mouth of the complaining party, glad to put his knowledge to the test. He was impatient with theory. He wanted to know how things worked, from the human body to the sailing ship. He studied printing, engineering, and shoemaking, disdaining no craft or trade; he labored in the shipyards of Amsterdam, dreaming of the day when Russia would have its own fleet. Back in Russia, Peter would later serve in

Peter the Great worked in the Amsterdam shipyards, dreaming of the day when Russia would have its own fleet. By the end of his reign, the Russian navy rivaled England on the seas.

both the army and the navy he was to create, starting at the very bottom and promoting himself only when he had mastered all the tasks and weapons of a given rank. His closest advisers were chosen exclusively on merit, a system that created some dizzying ascents: his closest associate, the notorious Alexander Menshikov, went from being a vendor of meat pies on Red Square to prince and then general, the equivalent of a sidewalk hot-dog man in Manhattan becoming governor of the state with scarcely a stop between.

Peter was practical to a fault. He had no use whatsoever for the Russia he had inherited, viewing its culture and religion only as obstructions to progress. He admired Ivan the Terrible for his achievement in creating a country that was independent, united, and mighty, but during the century that had passed since Ivan's death in 1584, the West had continued to surge ahead while Russia stood still, mired in mud and Muscovite custom.

There were, however, some signals of crises to come. The very beginning of the 16th century was marked by extreme chaos and violence caused by the lack of any clear successor to the throne. Finally, order was established and a new dynasty created: the Romanovs, who would rule Russia until the Revolution of 1917.

But nothing had been done about Russia's central problem—that the mass of the population had no stake in society; their voices were unheard, their needs never considered, their skills unused. They had more experience of being owned than of ownership. In fact, the Russian language even lacked the verb "to have." The peasants, who constituted 90 percent of the population, obeyed their rulers because they knew the price of disobedience, but they viewed the state as alien and hated the law as the masters' tool of oppression. Those of the peasants who could not bear the burden of serfdom, which had been codified into law in 1649, fled eastward to Siberia or south to the rich steppes. Successful farmers, they were always ready to mount their horses and defend their lives with their sabers. Their Tartar enemy gave them their name, Cossacks (from the Turkish word *Kazak*, meaning "free man"). The state did not impede their migration because it needed settlements along its underpopulated borders—especially in Siberia, where serfdom had never been introduced. Ironically, Siberia, a place that later came to signify exile and suffering both to Russia and the world, had an entirely different image then. It represented the freedom of wide-open spaces, where people could build the lives they wished.

But flight was only for the few, the bold. The overwhelming majority of Russian peasants accepted their lot, some humbly, most seething inwardly. Small eruptions of fury were common—a few dozen peasants, armed with axes and torches, would slaughter the lords and burn their manors—"letting out the red rooster," as such spontaneous arson was popularly known. But sometimes those local fires would ignite into a conflagration, as in 1670, when the Cossack Stenka Razin, whose name still lives in song, led an army of 20,000 up the Volga River proclaiming freedom for the people and death to the gentry. But Stenka Razin and his army lacked organization; the rebellion was cut down by the tsar's troops, and Razin was executed.

In the mid-1600s, the Russian Orthodox Church was rent by a deep schism that, as the historian Riasanovsky observes, was quite "the opposite of the Reformation: in the West, Christians turned against their ecclesiastical authorities because they wanted changes; in Russia, believers revolted because they refused to accept even minor modifications of the traditional religious usage." Those who rebelled identified the reforms with the oppressive, centralized Muscovite system, and tens of thousands of Russians preferred to burn themselves to death rather than make the sign of the cross with three fingers instead of the time-hallowed two. As often in Russia, fierce struggles for power focus on points of doctrine that strike outsiders as absurdly abstruse.

The hundred years between the death of Ivan the Terrible and the reign of Peter the Great were also marked by the gradual infiltration of Western ways and ideas. Foreigners were imported to process ore and build ironworks as well as run establishments manufacturing glass, gunpowder, and paper. Portraiture became popular in the land of the icon, and erotic tales of adventure gained currency even though Russian women were kept in seclusion. Some advanced Russians even cultivated roses and smoked tobacco, and the most daring among them went so far as to trim their beards—the very symbol of the Russian Orthodox faith. Russian statesman Pavel Miliukov calls the 17th century "essentially an age of transition, which lays the groundwork, and rapidly, for the reforms of Peter."

But it had not been rapid enough for Peter, a man in a hurry. There were not hours enough in the day for him to absorb all the technology the West had developed while his own country argued over how many fingers a true Christian should use when crossing himself. Then his limited time in Europe ran out. After about a year and a half of travel and work, word reached Peter that the elite guard of musketeers, who often played a crucial part in palace revolutions, had now risen against him. He dropped everything and dashed home in a fury.

Owing to the distance involved and the slowness of a horse-drawn carriage, the revolt had already been quashed by the time Peter returned. Yet he was not convinced that the musketeers had mutinied because of poor living conditions. He suspected a plot by his half-sister, who had previously displayed her lust for power. Fourteen torture chambers were constructed, as well as 30 furnaces in which the rebels were slowly roasted alive with Peter supervising every moment, ordering the doctors to revive those who had lost consciousness before confessing. In *Precursors of Peter the Great*, Zinaida Schakovskoy writes:

> After torture came the executions. Finding the headsman too slow at his job, Peter picked up the ax himself and sent his subjects' heads rolling to the dust, a royal giant with contorted features, foam-flecked lips and clothes stained with his victims' blood. Peter invited the foreigners in his service to help in the inquisition but [they] declined this peculiar honour on grounds that it would be inconsistent with their national code of behavior.

The heads of the rebels were impaled on spikes and displayed throughout Moscow, and—Peter's idea of a hint—195 men were hanged outside his sister's window. In Europe Peter had been a student of the West; at home he was a Russian tsar. It is typical of Peter's personal, hands-on style that he snatched the ax away from the executioner. But Peter was no Ivan. To him, violence was an instrument of state.

With the rebels dead and his sister confined to a monastery, Peter immediately plunged into his mission of reforming backward Russia. He personally cut off the beards of his courtiers and insisted that all officials and military personnel dress in Western style; only priests and peasants were exempt. Those wishing to retain their beards had to pay a special tax and produce the medallion issued them upon demand. In fact, Peter taxed everything in sight: beehives, mills, fisheries, bathhouses, stamped paper, oak coffins. He needed money to modernize his country and defeat its principal northern enemy, Sweden, which was still a great power at the end of the 17th century. Peter had no use for religion, and one of his favorite pastimes was to stage drunken orgies with blasphemous themes. Peter viewed religion as an ignorant superstition that would in time yield to reason's clear, dry light. Toward that end, he subordinated the Church to the state, an arrangement that lasted until the Revolution of 1917, when the new Soviet leaders decided the policy had been shamefully mild. Many of the deeply religious Russians saw in Peter nothing less than the coming of the Antichrist. Some conservative Russians still blame Peter for severing Russia's culture from its Christian roots and view him as a precursor to the antireligious terror of the Communists.

He saw himself as an enlightened despot, the first servant of the state. Riasanovsky remarks that "when reforming the army, Peter crossed out 'the interests of His Tsarist Majesty' as the object of military devotion and substituted 'the interests of the state.'" Peter was sincere in his belief that Russia had no choice but to become educated and modernized, and he would cut off the beard, or the head, of anyone who stood in the way.

Peter founded the first regular army and introduced the flintlock and bayonet. Overseeing the development of both light- and heavy-artillery units, he also took a hand in writing the military manuals. His efforts paid off. In 1709 Russia finally defeated its old rival Sweden in the Battle of Poltava in the Ukraine. Now Europe had to sit up and take notice. Russia had defeated a major Western power. There was a new force in the equation of continental politics.

But what Peter did with the army was nothing compared with what he accomplished in the fulfillment of his dream to build a Russian navy. Having started with one obsolete vessel, he left his country a formidable armada of 48 major warships and nearly 800 small craft, manned by 28,000 sailors. He had modeled his navy on the British fleet, but now the pupil was threatening his teacher; England had a new rival on the seas, and all Englishmen in the service of Russia were summoned home at once.

By 1721 Peter felt that he had earned the title of emperor, which the senate (a powerless body of his own creation) insisted he accept. As Ivan was the first tsar, Peter was the first emperor. His other firsts, however, make a more gratifying list than Ivan's. He created the first newspaper, the first public theater, the first hospital, and even an Academy of Sciences. Completed after Peter's death in 1725, the academy was an imposing structure. But despite Peter's titanic efforts, there were not enough scholars and scientists in Russia, so the staff had to be imported from abroad.

The most enduring symbol of Peter's legacy of Westernization is the city he commanded to be built on swampy terrain by the Gulf of Finland. Known variously in history as St. Petersburg, Petrograd, and Leningrad, it was always called simply Peter by those who lived there. St. Petersburg was to be both Russia's new capital and the point from which it could project its new naval power westward. Peter was unsparing in his use of the laborers he conscripted for the task. Thousands died, victims of the inhuman efforts required to perform construction in that hostile climate, which was marrow-chilling in winter, enervatingly humid in summer. A glittering European city rose on a foundation of bones.

Its architecture and canals were a mélange of Peter's European memories. St. Petersburg was both imposing and spectral; it existed for no other reason than having been ordered into being by the imperial will. Peter's method was described by Vladimir Weidlé in *Russia: Absent and Present*: ". . . western civilization was imposed on Russia from above, by decree, and with the frantic intransigence of a very raw genius."

Peter really had no choice. He had a vision of a Westernized Russia and the power to impose that vision. He knew that too much time had already been lost to wait for a gradual infiltration of Western influence that might never occur, given the stubborn resistance of the "longbeards," as he called them. Like Prince Vladimir and Ivan, Peter had to impose change from above, and the people, as always, remained silent, inert, and resentful. Peter had changed the direction of Russia's history but had failed to change the direction in which power flowed.

Peter the Great dominated the first half of 18th-century Russia, Catherine the Great the second half. The difference between their attitudes toward the West mirrors Russia's relationship to a civilization that it both fears and admires. Peter saw Western knowledge as a tool that could only strengthen the state; Catherine looked deeper and saw that Western knowledge was based on reasonable doubt, a force that could well be used to erode the authority of the state and challenge its very right to exist.

By birth a German princess of no particular prominence, Catherine married the heir to the Russian throne, Peter's grandson, Peter III. Becoming tsar, he soon alienated the nobility with his pro-Germany policies, while German Catherine was impressing them with her allegiance to Russian ways. With the nobility's assent, she had her lover kill her husband: a small price to pay to become empress of all Russia. Quite a liberated woman for those times, Catherine was very much taken by all the new thinking about laws, rights, and freedom that was in the air, especially in France.

Dynamic and intelligent, she wanted to continue Peter's Westernization of Russia. For inspiration she corresponded with Voltaire and the other leading figures of the Enlightenment. Wishing to recodify the legal system, she convened the Legislative Commission in 1767. A prolific writer, Catherine personally penned her *Instructions* for the delegates. The legal liberty she wished to grant the Russian people was so sweeping that *Instructions* was banned in France as too liberal.

But the rub was that to change the laws meant to change the society. And no one, least of all Catherine, was willing to face Russia's central problem—the serfs. The serf-owning gentry had

Catherine the Great (1729-1796), unlike Peter, realized that Western ideas could threaten the authority of the state.

backed her grab for power, and she could never have truly entertained any notion of depriving them of their rights and wealth. If anything, the position of the serfs worsened under Catherine, for all her progressive posturing on paper. Serfs were won and lost at cards, so low had their status sunk. Monstrous and grotesque excesses were commonplace. To take an example from a somewhat later time (but one that shows which way things were heading), the novelist Ivan Turgenev's mother refused to allow her household servants to have children. If any of the women became pregnant, they were forced to drown their newborns in the estate's pond, which every few years was raked clean of infant skeletons.

Catherine, that glorious hypocrite, formulated what was to become the classic justification for not liberating the serfs: the people's barbarity. As much as she would like to liberate them, how could she share power with illiterate peasants? In other words, the millions kept in ignorance could not be freed from it *because* of it.

Though she too neglected the essential domestic problems, Catherine succeeded mightily in war and diplomacy, adding amply to the empire by recapturing the lands that had originally formed Kievan Russia. All the while she indulged her prodigious sexual appetites, taking lover after lover, but usually not before they had been tried out by two ladies-in-waiting, who were familiar with Her Majesty's tastes and requirements.

If a scintilla of liberalism remained to Catherine, it vanished in 1773, when a Don Cossack named Emelyan Pugachev led a rebellion, promising the abolition of serfdom and calling for the slaughter of the landowners. The peasants responded, murdering with alacrity. Pugachev's army, 15,000 strong, came within 120 miles of Moscow before the regular army demonstrated the advantages of discipline over passion. Betrayed by his own lieutenants, Pugachev was taken to Moscow in a cage and executed. But his name would never die, haunting Catherine and all the tsars to come.

The next great shock for Catherine was the French Revolution in 1789. It was clear now that Western ideas could cost rulers not only their thrones but their heads. Thus, she was especially incensed in 1790, when a nobleman, Alexander Radishchev, published *A Journey From St. Petersburg to Moscow*, which described the horrific conditions in which the serfs lived and warned that inaction would have calamitous consequences. His solution was a republic and the emancipation of the serfs. "Worse than Pugachev!" exclaimed Catherine.

Taken together, the reigns of Catherine and Peter reveal an inherent contradiction in Russia's relation to the West. The fruits of Western civilization—reason, science, technology—grew on the tree of liberty over long years. Always behind, ever impatient, Russia wants those fruits but fears the tree and, in any case, lacks the soil in which it could flourish.

Still, both Peter and Catherine were grand successes—all that matters in history. Russia had been Westernized; the empire was still intact. It was now ready to assert its political presence on the world stage and to reveal the genius of its culture.

"his is how big the world looks to our tracking network."

Judy Paynter
Corporate Programs Administrator, Colorado Springs

Whether you're shipping computer parts to Cologne or machine tools to Milan, our
state-of-the-art tracking network enables us to pinpoint the precise location of your shipment
almost anywhere on earth, within seconds. Proving that it's a small world, after all.

5

THE 19TH CENTURY: PRELUDE TO REVOLUTION

The events of the Russian 19th century resemble what's happening in the U.S.S.R. today: an empire fails to solve social and political problems, and its structure collapses under its own weight. The fall of the tsarist empire led to Communism, Stalin, and the Cold War. Will the collapse of the Soviet empire produce consequences of similar magnitude?

In Russia, the 19th century opened with great hope and the shadow of murder. Tall, blond, and gentle of manner, the new tsar, Alexander I, was as bright as the century's new dawn. But it was also from him that the shadow fell. His father, Paul I, a crackpot despot who had forced the Russian army to dress in Prussian uniforms and sent Cossacks to attack India, had been strangled by courtiers in 1801. He was further proof of the adage that Russia's government was an absolute monarchy tempered by assassination. Alexander's exact role in his father's slaying is not known, but there is no question that the 23-year-old was morose and distracted at his coronation. Guilt wracked him all his life. "There is no cure for such a case as mine," he said. "I have to suffer. How is it possible that I should not suffer? Things will never change." Mysterious in life—he was known as the "enigmatic tsar," "the Sphinx," and "Hamlet with a crown"—he was mysterious in death as well. Perhaps he simply died suddenly from natural causes in 1825, perhaps he took his own life, or perhaps he didn't die then at all; maybe there is some truth to the legend that, unable to bear his sin any longer, he exchanged the bloody robes of power for the hermit's rags.

The young tsar had the noblest of visions, the best of intentions. He was clearly the one who could solve Russia's great problem: the unjust distribution of both wealth and liberty. All of his initial

Napoleon's Grand Army invaded Russia in 1812 and captured the Kremlin. When Moscow burned to the ground, Napoleon was forced to retreat before winter. But the first snows came early that year, with a vengeance.

actions indicated that Alexander wished to abolish autocracy and serfdom. Committees, formal and informal, convened to study various proposals, but in four years Alexander's only action was to pass a law allowing the gentry to emancipate their serfs if they so desired. A few did; most didn't.

By 1805 Alexander was facing a more immediate challenge. Napoleon had shattered the armies of Russia and Austria at the Battle of Austerlitz. A return engagement was inevitable, for now only two great powers were left on the European continent, Napoleon's and Alexander's, and Napoleon was a very ambitious man. Russia was about to learn that not only light came from the West, but death and destruction. The second great invasion of Russia began in June 1812, when Napoleon's Grand Army— 600,000 strong—surged into Lithuania. He may have been counting on Russia's technological backwardness, the dimensions of which were reflected by an Englishman's description, quoted in Virginia Cowles's *The Romanovs*, of a visit to a Russian arms factory in 1810: "The machinery is ill constructed and worse preserved. Workmen, with long beards, stood staring at each other, wondering what was to be done next; while their . . . directors were drunk or asleep." The muskets, "besides being clumsy and heavy . . . misfire five times out of six, and are liable to burst whenever discharged."

Alexander attempted to sue for peace. Napoleon would have none of it. Nothing impeded his progress from Lithuania to the city of Smolensk, the last stronghold protecting Moscow from the West. Alexander then appointed General Mikhail Kutuzov to command Russia's armies. Sixty-six, corpulent, blind in one eye from a war wound, Kutuzov spent his days as supreme commander dozing on a divan, his essential strategy being to let Napoleon overextend his supply lines. Finally he engaged Napoleon in the Battle of Borodino, 70 miles from Moscow. In one terrible day of fighting the Russians lost 42,000 men, the French 58,000. Though the Russian line had held, Kutuzov resumed his passive strategy of yielding ground. A week later, on September 14, 1812, Napoleon Bonaparte was the master of the Kremlin.

Supreme commander Mikhail Kutuzov's strategy for defending Russia in 1812 against Napoleon was to let him overextend his supply lines.

His victory soon turned to ashes, however, as Moscow went up in flames. The city either was put to the torch by the Russians or simply caught fire in the panic of evacuation. Napoleon had no choice but to withdraw before winter came. But winter came early that year, the first snows falling on November 4. Retreating over frozen land, raided by Cossacks and peasant guerrillas, the Grand Army withered away. Of the 600,000 that had entered Russia, no more than 50,000 left the country alive. The low point for Napoleon came in Lithuania, as described in the memoirs of General de Caulaincourt: "We had reached our destination . . . by a road that descended so steeply, that was so sunken, and a part of whose frozen surface had been so polished by the large number of horses and men who had slipped on it, that we were obliged like everyone else to sit down and let ourselves slide on our posteriors.

"We serve more gourmet meals than most restaurants."

James Mercurio
Account Executive, Dallas

Thanks to an innovative service called Dinners a la Federal Express,[sm] fine food merchants eager to expand their markets can ship anything from live lobsters to pecan pies, fresh to practically anywhere in the country. It's enough to satisfy even the heartiest new business appetites.

The Emperor had to do likewise. . . . "

Alexander had his revenge on March 31, 1814, when he led the Russian army into Paris. A hundred years earlier Peter the Great had gone there as a student; Alexander now came as a conqueror. It was Russia's turn to have an impact on France. Culinary legend even has it that the Russian officers, impatient to savor the pleasures of victory in Parisian restaurants, would frequently call out "Bistro, bistro!" (the Russian word for "quick"), thereby lending a Russian name to that most French of institutions.

But the officers who shared in Alexander's triumph and who had seen the splendors and liberties of the West soon grew disillusioned with their tsar, who had lost interest in reform and gradually became more mystical and reactionary. Soldiers and serfs suffered the consequences in the second half of Alexander's reign. The serfs were not yet ready to rise again, but a few officers were.

The tsar Alexander I (1777-1825) defeated Napoleon's Grand Army and marched into Paris as conqueror in 1814.

Alexander died, or disappeared, suddenly and mysteriously in 1825. On December 26 of that year, a handful of liberal revolutionaries, who came to be known as the Decembrists, took advantage of the confusion created by complications in the succession to the throne to stage a revolt in St. Petersburg. Their plan, according to Virginia Cowles, was "tragically amateurish." After a daylong standoff, the rebels were cut down, the survivors hanged or exiled. Nicholas I, the new tsar, demonstrated the iron will that would mark his entire reign. But a fateful line—the open defiance of tsarist authority—had been crossed. Martyrs were made, an example set.

Fearing revolution, Nicholas used censorship and the secret police to enforce obedience in thought and deed. A good Russian went to church, obeyed his tsar, and kept his mouth shut. The Polish uprising of 1830, an attempt to break free of the Russian empire, and the revolutions that swept Western Europe in 1848 only heightened Nicholas's ambition to be the gendarme of Europe. The rebellion in Poland was crushed, and Nicholas helped quell other empires' revolts.

In 1839 the Marquis de Custine, a French nobleman, traveled through Nicholas's Russia, and his account remains as valuable as de Tocqueville's of America: "I went to Russia in search of arguments against representative government. I returned from Russia a partisan of constitutions." He was not taken in by the splendors of St. Petersburg: "I do not blame the Russians for being what they are; I blame them for pretending to be what we are." He found Nicholas's government to have the "discipline of the camp substituted for civic order. . . . It is a state of siege become the normal state of society." Russia would have to "undergo a revolution more terrible than the revolution whose effects are still felt in Western Europe." Some of Custine's judgments were too harsh, but he understood an essential characteristic of that "predestined land": "Nothing is lacking in Russia . . . except liberty, that is to say life."

Keen observer though he was, Custine failed to detect the intellectual groundswell in Russia that was bringing a renaissance in literature and philosophy. In the early 19th century, with the emergence of the intelligentsia, Russia began asking new questions about itself: Who are we Russians? Do we belong to the East, the West, or neither? Where is Russia heading? Serfdom and the absence of political freedom also imposed a practical question: What is to be done?

Those questions persisted throughout the 19th century and contributed to the passion that marked the golden age of literature between 1820 and 1881: the works of Pushkin, Gogol, Turgenev, Tolstoy, and Dostoyevsky. Two schools of thought emerged—the Westernizers, who believed that Russia would do best by modeling itself on European civilization; and the Slavophiles, who held that Russia was a civilization unto itself with its own historical path to follow. That debate reaches to the present, shaping the battle between those who favor political democracy and a market economy, and those who find them unsuitable for Russia, either because of philosophical principle or because they fear that competition would cost them power and privilege.

Backed by the secret police, Tsar Nicholas I ruled with an iron will.

In 1854, Nicholas I led his country into the calamitous Crimean War. Fought in the southern reaches of the empire, the war exposed Russia as a helpless giant, unable to supply its own troops on its own soil, defeated by its own distances. The only significant railroad in the country was the Moscow-Petersburg line, running as perfectly straight through the countryside as the line that the impatient Nicholas had drawn on the map when his engineers had squabbled over the best route. Russia, behind again, had failed the test of war.

Nicholas died during the war and was succeeded by his son, Alexander II, who drew this hard lesson from the Crimean War: serfdom was not only unjust, it was inefficient. The serfs made neither good farmers nor good soldiers; why should they work hard and die for their masters? Moving slowly but decisively to override the gentry's objections, Alexander issued the Emancipation Manifesto on March 3, 1861, which freed the serfs two years before Lincoln freed the slaves, thereby earning himself the title of "Tsar-Liberator." In short order, he democratized local govern-

Alexander II was assassinated in 1881, when terrorists bombed his carriage on the streets of St. Petersburg.

ment and created a separate judiciary. Trial by jury was introduced for serious crimes. All Russians were now equal before the law. "Almost overnight," writes Riasanovsky, this change "transformed the Russian judiciary from one of the worst to one of the best in the civilized world." A courageous leader had saved Russia. Or so it seemed.

Russia of the 1860s was ill prepared to absorb change, which, as always, came from the top. The country had no middle class, no social or psychological middle ground where realistic compromises could be worked out. The peasants had been freed and received land, but Alexander had also decreed that the peasants must pay for the property. Usually allotted the least productive land, they were hard-pressed to make the payments. They had gone from one bondage to another, confirming their long-held belief that the law was only an instrument of oppression. The simple, extreme conditions of Russian life—a wealthy elite, the masses living in squalor and misery—and the old tendency to favor the simple solutions of the "one truth" quickly produced a small but dedicated and dangerous revolutionary class. Like Peter the Great, the revolutionaries wanted to obliterate the past and start with a clean slate. The early radicals were typically "repentant nobles"—that is, people born to wealth and position whose conscience would allow them no peace as long as the overwhelming majority of the nation suffered in poverty. Later, revolutionaries began to emerge from the lower-middle class—the children of priests, petty officials, tradesmen. Selfless, pure, willing to die for their ideals, they were equally willing to kill for them.

Only five years after the emancipation, a student made the first attempt on the life of Alexander II. More attempts followed; a huge bomb even rocked the Winter Palace. The emperor hunt was on, and Alexander, who had given Russia more freedom and justice than it had ever known, cried out in heartbroken amazement: "But why on earth are all those wretched men against me? Am I a wild animal to be hounded to the death?"

Perhaps it is the fate of liberators like Lincoln and Alexander to be struck down. In any case, bomb-hurling assassins caught up with the Tsar-Liberator on March 13, 1881. After the first bomb was hurled, the tsar emerged from his carriage and, seeing that none of his guards had been killed, exclaimed, "Thank God!" A second terrorist replied, "A little too early to be thanking God," and hurled a bomb that tore off the tsar's leg and split open his torso. Alexander died a few hours later. The timing could not have been worse; left on Alexander's desk was an edict proclaiming limited representative government in Russia.

It would have taken a saint or an exceedingly enlightened ruler to heed Tolstoy's plea to grant clemency to the assassins. The new tsar, Alexander III, was neither. His father's killers were hanged, the edict torn to pieces. Russia was now in for 13 years of brutal repression. Physically strong and mentally weak, Alexander decided that the Jews were responsible for much of Russia's troubles because the assassins had used a Jewish woman's apartment for their conspiracy. "We must never forget that it was the Jews who crucified our Lord and spilled His priceless blood," said the new tsar. Alexander III proclaimed laws confining Jews to the Pale of Settlement in western Russia; he closed Jewish schools and forbade the printing of books in Hebrew. Pogroms broke out; within six months more than 250,000 of Russia's five million Jews left the country in an exodus that would increase as the violence against them worsened. Some went to Western Europe, many to America.

"Beat the Jews and save Russia!" later became the rallying cry for pogroms by fascist groups such as the Black Hundreds. But beating Jews would not save Russia. The real problem was that the majority of the population was still exploited by the few and might yet rise in revolt. Terrorists tried to incite that revolt. In 1887 a young student named Alexander Ulyanov was arrested and executed for his involvement in a plot to kill the tsar. One can only imagine the effect his hanging would have on his 17-year-old brother, Vladimir, soon known to the world as Lenin.

By the end of the 19th century, Russia seemed to be an infernal contraption designed to self-destruct. Industrialization had come late; now, trying to make up for lost time, thousands of miles of railroad track were laid and factories were built to exploit the land's natural resources—coal, iron, gold. So much foreign capital was required that the Marxists, the dominant radicals in the 1890s, spoke derisively of Russia's "semi-colonial" status. This industrialization, however, spawned the proletariat that Marx said was essential to revolution, and, as if to prove him right, the Russian capitalists cruelly exploited the workers. Strikes broke out in St. Petersburg by the late 1870s. The tsarist government had no new ideas for handling social crisis. They preached only old nationalist slogans, which had less meaning than ever in the multinational empire that reached from Finland to Central Asia.

Marxism and Darwinism fell on fertile soil in Russia. Many of the young revolutionaries embraced both philosophies, each of which taught that life was struggle. But the class struggle, the revolution—"Give us an organization of revolutionaries, and we shall overturn the whole of Russia!" as Lenin put it—seemed doomed to reveries of utopia and vengeance as long as Alexander III was in charge. In 1894 he died of natural causes at age 49 and was succeeded by his 26-year-old son, Nicholas II.

Now begins the dark and tragic fairy tale that is the end of the Romanov dynasty, the end of tsardom in Russia. Vacillating and ungifted, Nicholas wept over his father's death not only from grief but also because he knew he was unfit to be a ruler (one of his rare accurate insights). He most likely would have been happier as a grand duke, commanding a ceremonial regiment or vacationing with his family on the royal yacht. But, a dutiful son, he continued his father's reactionary policies.

Those policies became increasingly irrelevant. As industrialization accelerated, labor strikes spread, and their suppression became more violent. By now the Marxists had able leaders—Lenin, Trotsky, and, waiting in the wings for his moment to come, Stalin. In 1903 Lenin had broken with the other revolutionaries and formed his own party, the Bolsheviks.

As the age of the tsars came to a close, Russian culture enjoyed a last phosphorescent brilliance. There was a resurgence of poetry, music, ballet, theater, painting, and philosophy—a period known as the Silver Age. The Russian spirit soared, but its flight was feverish, frenetic. One of the great poets of the time, Alexander Blok, claimed he could literally hear the collapse of tsardom.

The collapse was hastened by the Russo-Japanese War of 1904-5. Russia's eastward expansion, partly driven by a search for new markets for products that had no buyers in the West, brought Russia into collision with Japan. Nicholas thought nothing would restore Russia's patriotic vigor like a "short, victorious" war.

Short it was. Japan, which had gone from swords to battleships in half a century, destroyed the Russian fleet in two major engagements. It was the humiliation of the Crimean War all over again.

As the defeats piled up, the country erupted in more strikes and assassinations, and not in patriotism, as Nicholas had hoped. On January 22, 1905, a day that would go down in history as Russia's Bloody Sunday, a delegation of workers carrying icons and led by a priest proceeded to the Winter Palace to petition their tsar for a redress of grievances. They were met not by the tsar but by police, who killed 130 workers and wounded hundreds more. On that day the ancient contract between tsar and people was broken, putting to rest the belief that all would be well if only the tsar knew the truth.

Russia was in revolution. The sailors of the battleship *Potemkin* mutinied and turned their big guns on their own land. The peasants rampaged, and the workers of St. Petersburg formed executive councils known as soviets to coordinate a strike that so paralyzed the country that even Nicholas had to face facts. On the last day of the 18-day strike, October 30, 1905, he issued the October Manifesto, which granted Russians civil liberties and allowed the creation of a genuine legislature. For all intents and purposes, Russia was now a constitutional monarchy.

But Nicholas did not keep his bargain with the nation. He retained as much power for himself as he could, thwarting the legislature, known as the Duma, making it a sham. Meanwhile, police spies were everywhere, and revolutionaries were being arrested and exiled. By some terrible twist, Russia had less liberty than ever.

If the small disastrous war with Japan had generated the inconclusive revolution of 1905, it would probably take a huge disastrous war to generate a successful revolution. In August 1914, Russia and the world stumbled into that war. Once again Russia was ill prepared, technologically behind. Defeat followed defeat, and for a time in 1915 a quarter of Russia's soldiers were sent into battle unarmed and told to pick up weapons from the dead. In that same year Nicholas appointed himself commander in chief, leaving affairs of state to his wife, Alexandra, who was under the spell of Rasputin, an unsavory but gifted psychic who was able to treat the tsarevitch's hemophilia. In December 1916, Rasputin was murdered, but it took poison, knives, bullets, and finally drowning to kill him. By then the soldiers of the Russian army were using the weapons they picked up from the dead against their own officers. They mutinied in droves, only to find upon returning home that their families were freezing and starving. Riots broke out in the capital, and the troops sent to subdue them joined their ranks. Realizing that he no longer had authority, Nicholas abdicated. For the first time since Ivan the Terrible, Russia was not ruled by a tsar.

In fact, Russia was not ruled much at all in the six months between Nicholas's abdication and the seizure of power by the Bolsheviks in October of that same year, 1917. Alexander Kerensky became the final leader of the Provisional Government that was to preside until general elections could be held. He was derisively known as the "persuader in chief," for neither the police nor the army would back up his orders. The peasants wanted peace and land, but Kerensky did not feel sufficiently empowered either to pull Russia out of the war or to redistribute the land. It was a period of dual power with the real authority held by the soviets, executive councils that controlled a given garrison, factory, or city block.

Lenin, who understood power the way a physicist understands weights and pressures, saw that the soviets were the fulcrum on which he could overturn the Provisional Government and with it all of Russia. He launched his famous slogan—All power to the soviets—though what he in fact meant was all power to his party, the Bolsheviks. After sporadic fighting on November 7, Bolshevik-led troops stormed the Winter Palace, weakly defended by young cadets and a battalion of women. The remainder of the Provisional Government was arrested; Kerensky had already fled. It was a remarkably bloodless exercise: only five men were killed in the taking of the palace. The blood, in torrents, would flow later.

"Even if I can't lift your shipment, I can still pick it up."

Kin Wong
Courier, Taipei, Taiwan

At Federal Express, we'll pick up and deliver big shipments as well as small ones. In fact, when it comes to international air freight, we carry more weight than anyone in the industry. Something which should give a big lift to shippers everywhere.

CHAPTER
6

LENIN'S TOMB, STALIN'S GHOST

Communism today is a dead faith. Yet many Russians still cling to it because it gives them power and privilege, or simply because it is a known quantity. Certainly it no longer inspires the grand visions it once did.

"The average human type will rise to the heights of an Aristotle, a Goethe, or a Marx. And above this ridge new peaks will rise," wrote Leon Trotsky at the conclusion of his book *Literature and Revolution*. Vision and violence were directly correlated in the Communist mentality; after all, anyone standing in the way of their great dream must indeed be the enemy of mankind. They foresaw revolution sweeping Russia, Europe, and the world, establishing societies so free and just that the police and the state would wither away, people having matured enough to govern themselves. As we know, nothing of the sort occurred. What took place instead was ably summarized by the Russian novelist and critic Andrei Sinyavsky in his book *On Socialist Realism*: "So that prisons should vanish forever, we built new prisons. So that all frontiers should fall, we surrounded ourselves with a Chinese Wall. So that work should become a rest and a pleasure, we introduced forced labor. So that not one drop of blood be shed anymore, we killed and killed and killed."

What caused this tragic paradox? A good deal of the answer lies in four fateful decisions that led to the downfall of the Bolshevik Revolution and the ascent of Joseph Stalin. The first was made only six weeks after Lenin and the Bolsheviks seized power. On December 20, 1917, he created the Soviet secret police, the Cheka. The Cheka's mandate was to employ "organized terror" against all enemies of the revolution and Bolshevik power, which were identical in Lenin's mind.

The Bolsheviks allowed the elections that had been promised by the Provisional Government after the deposition of the last tsar. The Russians voted overwhelmingly for parties on the far left. The Bolsheviks, however, placed a distant second. Lenin confronted a stark choice: accept the vote and lose power, or reject the elections. The new legislature, known as the Constituent Assembly, met exactly once, in January 1918. Using armed sailors, Lenin shut it down the next day.

Meanwhile, the war with Germany was still being waged—and still being lost. In March 1918 the Germans advanced on Petrograd, forcing Lenin to move the capital to Moscow. The same month, Soviet Russia negotiated a peace with Germany that cost it the Ukraine, Poland, Finland, Lithuania, Estonia, and Latvia. A quarter of its population (60 million), one-fourth of its arable land, and three-quarters of its steel industries and coal fields had been lost.

No sooner had Russia concluded peace with Germany than it was at war again, and this time civil war. Bolshevik Reds were attacked by the counterrevolutionary armies, known as the Whites. They were composed of landowners, tsarist officers, and the middle class—all of whom had everything to lose. They were also joined by revolutionaries who saw Lenin as more dangerous than the restoration of the tsar. The Whites knew that if they were led by the tsar himself, they would have a significantly better chance of defeat-

Lenin's Bolshevik Reds were shot down in Petrograd while trying to flee the White armies' machine-gun fire during the Russian Revolution in 1917.

Tsar Nicholas II and his family were executed by the Bolsheviks in 1918, ending the White armies' hopes of restoring tsardom.

ing the Reds. This remained a possibility, as long as Tsar Nicholas II, Alexandra, and the royal family were still alive, even though held captive in Ekaterinburg (now Sverdlovsk), just east of the Ural Mountains in Siberia. On the morning of July 17, 1918, an execution squad put the entire royal family to death.

The Russian civil war was as formless as it was vicious. Towns changed hands a dozen times, people never knowing under whose control they would be the next morning or whose retribution they would have to face. Nothing resembling a front line was ever established. The Whites had large armies in the east and south, but their actions were uncoordinated. The Reds had the advantage of holding the heartland, the area around Moscow, which was also the country's industrial center. Trotsky had proved a brilliant military organizer, building the Red Army out of former tsarist officers and working-class soldiers. The Cheka remained powerful, executing those suspected of siding with the Whites. Most important, the Reds had the rage of centuries on their side.

By the end of 1920, the White armies had been driven out of the country. Soviet Russia had peace, but it had been nearly destroyed by war. Combat, epidemics, executions, and starvation had cost Russia approximately 20 million lives. Industrial production fell 80 percent from the pre–World War I level. Famine struck in the first year of peace, and cannibalism was common. Those who dropped dead in the streets were quickly stripped of any flesh left on them.

Even the radical proletariat began to turn against the Bolsheviks, whose name now inspired such hatred that they changed it to Communists. Word magic didn't help. The country was in crisis, on the verge of yet another revolution. The sailors of the Baltic fleet, stationed on the island of Kronstadt, revolted. Legendary for their heroism during the revolution, the sailors demanded that power go back to the soviets—those local councils of workers, peasants, and military—and that the freely elected Constituent Assembly be reconvened. Lenin was now faced with his third agonizing choice: accede to the sailors' demands and lose power, or slaughter the finest sons of the revolution. He sent Trotsky with an army across the ice to do the job.

After suppressing the rebellion, Lenin made peace with the Russian people. The "peace treaty" took the form of the New Economic Policy (NEP), which put a stop to the seizure of grain supplies, allowing the peasants to sell their produce and to pay taxes in kind; in other words, private farming was again permitted. And it was soon successful. Small-scale capitalism was also allowed in the manufacture, distribution, and sales of other goods, though the state retained control of banking, big industry, transportation, and foreign trade. In fact, the NEP approach was similar to what Gorbachev is trying to implement today, with two important differences: in the 1920s Russia still had many experienced business people, and those venturing into private enterprise today know their history well enough to remember what a bad end—exile, arrest, execution—awaited all those entrepreneurs of the NEP era.

Lenin's fourth fateful choice was made during the same party congress in 1921 that made NEP official policy. To ensure the survival of the party, Lenin rammed through a piece of legislation—a loophole—allowing members to be expelled for opposing the party line. Having seen how his party was nearly torn in two over the Kronstadt incident, Lenin realized that the greatest danger to Communist rule was dissent within the party. If the party

"Using Federal Express to distribute Sharp® parts was a sharp idea."

Conrad Westerman
Federal Express Warehouse Manager, Memphis

Recently, Sharp Electronics started using our Memphis-based Business Logistics Services
division for the storage and distribution of important office
equipment parts. And quickly discovered that they could cut both warehousing
costs. *And* delivery time. Quite sharply.

divided, its members could be swept out of power and left to the mercy of the Russian people, who had tolerated their decrees only because they were enforced with the terror of the Cheka.

Lenin's four fateful choices had now given Stalin everything he needed to seize power. A secret police had been established, popular democracy had been crushed by disbanding the Constituent Assembly, the essential spirit of the revolution had been violated in the suppression of the Kronstadt uprising, and a means of seizing power had been created by Lenin's legislative loophole. All that stood between Stalin and absolute power were Lenin and Trotsky. A debilitating stroke eliminated Lenin, only 51 years old, in mid–1922.

As Lenin's condition worsened, he realized that a struggle over his successor between Trotsky and Stalin was inevitable. He wrote a final testament containing his instructions for succession, to be read to the party upon his death. Lenin favored Trotsky.

Leon Trotsky lost his bid for power after Lenin's death. His rival, Stalin, exiled him in 1929; in 1940 Stalin had Trotsky assassinated in Mexico City.

Trotsky was taking a health cure in the south when Lenin died on January 21, 1924. Stalin, using the simplest of dirty tricks, telegraphed Trotsky that the funeral would be the next day. He implied that the distance between Moscow and the Black Sea would make Trotsky's absence inevitable. Amazingly, Trotsky, who was commissar of war at the time, did not use his own channels to learn that the funeral would not, in fact, be held for several days. His lack of suspicion would cost him everything.

Stalin stole the show at the funeral, delivering the oration and making the most of Trotsky's insulting absence. Stalin also overrode all objections and ordered Lenin's body embalmed and a mausoleum erected on Red Square. Lenin, who favored the Bolshevik style—plain, brusk, severe—would have been sickened by such idolatry. But Stalin knew what he was doing; he was creating Soviet icons to sanctify the revolution and, ultimately, himself. The paradox facing the leader today is that to remove Lenin's body from the tomb would be in accord with what Lenin would have wished; yet that act would strike at the sanctity of the revolution and undermine Communist authority. Stalin outwitted not only his contemporaries but his successors as well.

Stalin did not, strictly speaking, seize power. He moved slowly and cautiously, taking five years to complete what one of his biographers, Boris Souvarine, termed a "molecular *coup d'état.*" With utter contempt, Trotsky accused Stalin of being a mere "committee man." Stalin must have smiled behind his mustache, accepting that accusation as a compliment. No match for Trotsky in intellect or speaking ability, Stalin understood that if he could control a majority of the party committees, he could in time garner enough votes to use Lenin's loophole against Trotsky. Finally Stalin accused Trotsky of opposing the party—just what Lenin feared most. Stalin sliced away at Trotsky's power a year at a time, removing him from his post as commissar of war, expelling him from the Politburo, then the party, then from Moscow, and finally, in 1929, from the Soviet Union. By the time Stalin turned 50 in December 1929, he was in complete control, and Russia was to suffer as it never had before.

To the relief of many Communists, Stalin immediately put an end to the New Economic Policy, that capitalistic smirch on Bolshevik honor. Businessmen were exiled, arrested, executed; yesterday's virtue was today's crime.

The two pillars of Stalin's domestic policies were industrialization and collectivization, bland words that would conceal immense and heinous crimes. Surrounded by hostile foreign powers— "capitalist encirclement" was the official term used—Soviet Russia needed heavy industry and needed it fast. Through his rapid introduction of slave labor, Stalin removed his enemies from circulation and put them to work constructing roads, factories, and canals.

Collectivization meant establishing gigantic agricultural enterprises that were controlled by the state. Whether this was a better way to grow food was irrelevant. The peasants had to be subordinated because their natural conservatism, their age-old distrust of the state and the city, could lead them to withhold food. A new decree proclaimed that private farmers were to surrender their seed, livestock, and equipment and join collective farms. The wealthy peasants, the kulaks, however, were to be "liquidated as a class," a phrase that made mass-murder sound like gerrymandering. Tanks and bombers were used against anyone who resisted. The *coup de grâce* was an artificial famine in the Ukraine. Grain was seized, roads blocked, the peasants left to starve. Scholars still debate how many millions died, but as Stalin remarked, "One death is a tragedy, a million a statistic."

Stalin controlled the statistics and the media; headlines celebrated bumper crops in the Ukraine while starvation and cannibalism were rampant. When he had succeeded with industrialization and collectivization, Stalin launched the Great Terror that sent millions to the gulag (if they were lucky). He saw enemies everywhere and, by a certain mad logic, he was right, for the more people he killed, the more people wished him dead. No one was safe, not even the

This scene from a Soviet World War II documentary film shows the Red Army advancing against the Nazis at Stalingrad.

heads of the secret police, who fell one after the other, as if it were they alone who had been responsible for all the bloody excesses. Old Bolsheviks and associates of Trotsky were particularly likely to be thrown into execution cellars; a quick bullet behind the right ear was now Stalin's way of doing politics.

The terror reached its hideous apogee in 1937. In June of that year, the Red Army's leading generals were arrested, tried for treason, and immediately executed. A decimating purge of the officer class ensued. Stalin feared there might be a Bonaparte among them, and though Hitler's Germany posed a real threat to Stalin, he preferred to destroy his most gifted military leaders rather than risk their turning against him in the event of a war against Nazi Germany. As usual, Stalin's logic led to execution.

In August 1939, after a decade of anti-Nazi propaganda, Stalin and Hitler suddenly became allies and the Molotov-Ribbentrop Pact was signed. The agreement promised nonaggression and mutual economic assistance (Russian raw materials for German finished goods) and contained secret clauses for dividing all the territory that lay between the two countries. On September 1, 1939, Hitler attacked Poland, and on September 17, as per the agreement, the Red Army occupied the eastern half of that tragic land. What Stalin failed to notice was that Germany and the Soviet Union now had a common border, Hitler having advanced several hundred miles east with Stalin's unwitting connivance. Stalin, who could detect danger where there was none, was blind to the real threat.

By June 1941 the German-Soviet border extended from the Baltic to the Black Sea, and there was an immense Nazi army amassed there. Hitler dispensed with the formalities of *casus belli* and a declaration of war. On June 22, 1941, a German army with 4.6 million soldiers, 5,000 planes, and 3,700 tanks invaded Soviet Russia. The Soviet air force was almost entirely destroyed on the ground during the opening hours of the war. The German strategy was the blitzkrieg, a three-pronged lightning bolt aimed simultaneously at Leningrad, the base of industry; Moscow, the seat of government; and Kiev, the capital of the fertile Ukraine. The Germans planned a quick victory, the three key cities to fall before the first autumn rains turned Russia to mud. The Germans slashed through ill-prepared and ill-equipped Russian armies. Kiev fell, Leningrad was surrounded, and the first German soldiers appeared in the far outskirts of Moscow, a few bombs even cratering Red Square. But Russian valor, German arrogance—Hitler had equipped his soldiers for victory, not winter—and early snows deprived Germany of swift victory. Moscow resisted two German onslaughts in late 1941, and though severed from the rest of the country, Leningrad did not fall.

Russia now dismantled much of its industry and sent it by rail beyond the Ural Mountains to Siberia, where factories were soon producing formidable tanks and artillery. Much of the government was relocated to Kuibyshev, a city on the Volga River; even Lenin's body was shipped there for safekeeping. Stalin, however, remained in Moscow, which gave the nation heart. In radio addresses he called for "death to the invader," whom he likened to Napoleon. Stalin knew how to play on Russian patriotism.

Leningrad was under siege, shelled constantly, deprived of supplies. By the winter of 1941, the city had no heat or electricity. People walked miles to work 12 hours in freezing factories where they were fed starvation rations. Cats and dogs disappeared. People simply expired at their desks, on the streets, at home in a chair; 10,000 people died every day during the worst of it. But the city held even after 900 days of siege.

In the summer of 1942, Hitler overextended his armies again, grabbing for both the oil fields near the Black Sea and the rail nexus of Stalingrad, where a victory would have had both strategic and symbolic value. Stalin issued his orders: "Not a step back." But the Germans took Stalingrad, although it quickly became a deathtrap for them. The city had been reduced to a rubble that made tanks useless; the battle became one between men instead of machines. The battle during the winter of 1942 was carried out street by street, building by building, floor by floor. The Russians were dressed for the murderous cold; the Germans, astonishingly, were not. In January 1943, reduced to eating the brains of dead horses, the Germans surrendered.

Stalingrad was the spiritual turning point of the war, the great tank battle of Kursk that summer the swing point of military fortune. Each side had about 3,000 tanks, and as they closed in battle, German superiority in the air became meaningless. The Soviet tanks could take more punishment, and mete out more as well. When the smoke cleared, the German war machine had essentially been defeated. Now it was victory after victory for the Red Army; now the cry was "On to Berlin!" In effect, Germany's fate had been decided before the Americans even hit the beaches at Normandy. Russia had done the real killing and the real dying.

For decades the official number of Soviet war dead, military and civilian, would be given as 20 million, a figure with a tragic aura like that of the six million Jewish victims of the Holocaust. But then suddenly, in the late 1980s, Gorbachev and his military leaders began using a new, updated figure: 27 million. The vastness of Russia and its suffering are in that disparity: a misplaced New York City's-worth of the dead.

Having saved the country for Stalin, the Russians expected life to be better after the war. In that hope, as in so many others, they were deceived. Grief and the hardships of rebuilding the country had to be borne in silence. Informers were everywhere. Some people denounced neighbors out of hysteria, others for practical advantage. One way to get a room in this time of housing shortages was to report a tenant to the secret police for telling an anti-Stalin joke or having contact with a foreigner. Stalin's worst legacy is the erosion of all trust. Russians fear each other to this day.

The Cold War began almost immediately after the end of World War II, Stalin no longer having any need for his capitalist allies. By 1948 Andrei Sakharov and other patriotic scientists had given Russia the H-bomb. Stalin, numerically the greatest murderer of all time, was now in possession of the greatest weapon of all time.

After Stalin's death in 1953, Nikita Khrushchev won the scramble for power. His political policy was anti-Stalinism, his social program fairly liberal reform. But Khrushchev's 11-year reign was highly erratic. He opened the gates of the gulag and in 1956 gave his famous "secret speech" in which he accused Stalin of monstrous crimes. Yet, in that same year he crushed the Hungarian uprising, demonstrating the limits of the new tolerance. He allowed Solzhenitsyn to publish *One Day in the Life of Ivan Denisovich*, a novel that laid bare the world of Stalin's camps, but hounded Boris Pasternak both for publishing *Doctor Zhivago* abroad and for daring to question the value of the revolution. Stalin had allowed a resurgence of Christianity to fuel the flames of patriotism during the war, but Khrushchev's oppression of religion recalled the 1930s. In one year alone, 1961, Khrushchev sent the first man into space, built the Berlin Wall, and, under cover of night, had Stalin's body slipped out of Lenin's tomb. The following year, he brought the world to the brink of nuclear war in the Cuban Missile Crisis. In October 1964 he was informed by the Politburo that, because of his various "harebrained" schemes involving agriculture and party reform, he was out of a job. He was pensioned off, though, rather than executed—a good sign. The Stalin era was over. Death was no longer the cost of political defeat.

Nikita Khrushchev succeeded Stalin. An erratic ruler, he brought the world to the brink of nuclear war in the Cuban Missile Crisis of 1962.

The Khrushchev years are typically referred to as the "thaw," but they were really more of a January thaw, a benign mildness that precedes the next cold snap. The new leadership of Leonid Brezhnev was devoted to reimposing limits. Writers and other intellectuals who had grown too daring during the heady Khrushchev years were arrested, exiled, or declared mad and sent to mental hospitals. The cult of Stalin was renewed. His body was buried immediately to the left of Lenin's tomb, and a large bust was erected upon the grave. Czechoslovakia was invaded in 1968 when the Kremlin decided that Prague's reforms were becoming insubordination.

Also in 1968, Andrei Sakharov, father of the Soviet H-bomb, made his decisive break from the establishment with his essay *Reflections on Progress, Peaceful Coexistence, and Intellectual Freedom. The New York Times* published it in its entirety, and it was soon circulating in the Soviet underground press (*samizdat*). Sakharov had fired the first salvo in the war between society and state that would define the Soviet '70s. His central idea was clear and challenging: "The key to international security is trust, which depends on a society's openness and respect for human rights." In other words, only the democratization of Russia could save the world from the nuclear-arms race. A few brave men and women, known as the Dissidents, attempted to make the Soviet government abide by Soviet law and the Soviet constitution, which granted citizens any number of rights. Those rights, however, were not to be exercised. When the Soviet Union invaded Afghanistan in late December 1979, Andrei Sakharov was one of the few Soviets who protested, calling the invasion a "major blunder." He was exiled to the closed city of Gorky, where he would remain until the Soviet Union acknowledged he had been right.

After the death of Brezhnev and his two short-lived successors, Yuri Andropov and Konstantin Chernenko, Mikhail Gorbachev became the Soviet leader in March 1985. Though Margaret Thatcher called the urbane Gorbachev a man one "could do business with," during his first two years he produced few hard signs of real change: Soviet troops remained in Afghanistan and Sakharov remained in exile. Gorbachev's slogans of *glasnost* ("openness") and *perestroika* ("rebuilding") sounded encouraging, but his hand had actually been forced by events: Chernobyl had blown the first hole in the iron curtain, and the unsuccessful war in Afghanistan had revealed the system's flaws. There were also questions about Gorbachev's political sincerity. After all, he had joined the Communist Party in 1952, when Stalin was still alive, and had come up through the stifling Soviet bureaucracy. Moreover, he was the protégé of Andropov, the longtime head of the KGB. But that also meant that Gorbachev was privy to KGB intelligence. As the best-informed government agency, the KGB knew exactly how far behind other industrialized nations Russia had slipped economically and technologically during the years of the Brezhnev "stagnation." The KGB had apparently reached the conclusion that information was the lifeblood of technology and had to circulate freely; democracy was the price of progress. That could not have made them very happy.

Andrei Sakharov, father of the Soviet H-bomb and leader of the human-rights movement, was exiled to Gorky in 1980 for protesting the invasion of Afghanistan.

Suddenly, in late 1987, Mikhail Gorbachev began astonishing the world, his nation, and perhaps himself as well. He released Sakharov, freed political prisoners, began withdrawing from Afghanistan, and allowed a dizzying freedom of debate. The first free elections since 1917 created a genuine if imperfect parliament. Sakharov went from being an enemy of the people to a Deputy of the People. NEP-like private business was allowed. Books banned for decades were suddenly in print. The removal of Lenin's body was called for on national television. Then the terrible Armenian earthquake of December 1988 exposed the shoddiness of Soviet architecture, the weakness of the infrastructure, the low quality of emergency medical aid (glass bottles of blood plasma with rags for stoppers). The Soviet Union was revealed as a third-world country with nuclear weapons and a space program.

Shaken by the earthquakes of history, the Soviet empire proved no more shock-resistant than the buildings of Armenia. The satellites—Poland, Czechoslovakia, Hungary, and East Germany—had been subordinated by the threat of force. In autumn 1989, gambling that tanks would not be used against them, they broke free with stunning ease, because neither loyalty nor self-interest bound them to Moscow. Once the spell of authority was broken, even the Berlin Wall was breached. A death zone became a dance floor.

But champagne gives the worst hangovers. All too soon it became clear that the collapse of the Soviet empire could be even more dangerous than the Cold War. A stable Russia with its missiles aimed at a distant enemy is one thing; a Russia spinning in chaos with those missiles is quite another. The world has seen empires come and go, but the fall of a nuclear empire is unprecedented.

"Our planes may deliver the shipments. But I deliver the planes."

Jim Simmons
Lead Mechanic, Chicago

One reason why our planes do such an outstanding job is because
our mechanics do such an outstanding job. In fact, over the years, we've managed
to maintain an on-time performance record that's the envy of every scheduled airline.
Which explains why nobody delivers like Federal Express.

7

TOMORROW
AND TOMORROW

Most change in Russia, from Christianity to *glasnost*, has been imposed from above. In recent times it was a handful of dissidents, not the Russian people, who were clamoring for freedom. It remains unclear how the Russian masses will act at the critical hour. Will they still favor cradle-to-grave security over the chanciness of the free market? Will they prize order over the creative confusions of democracy? Have they been so damaged by a century of evil and suffering that they no longer believe in anything, themselves least of all? How they act, or do not act, will determine whether their country will be reborn in peace or in violence.

What is clear is that their legendary patience has now worn thin. Better informed than ever before, the Russians are not happy with what they're hearing. They find it galling to learn, for example, that in 1990 somewhere between 30 percent and 60 percent of all produce never reached the marketplace; it fell off trucks and rotted in the open air for lack of storage. The country faces staggering problems—the feeble infrastructure, the artificial pricing system, and antiquated communications: Soviet executives' desks are still covered by a score of different-colored telephones. The business class was wiped out in the late 1920s, when NEP was halted. The best farmers were exterminated by Stalin in the early 1930s. Russia had been a grain-exporting nation before the revolution. The collective farms sapped initiative by equally rewarding the lazy and the industrious.

Drunkenness remains the national pastime. Gorbachev utterly failed to wean his people from the "hard drink" of which Prince Vladimir complained a thousand years ago. Passivity is a national trait that long predates the Soviet era, and one that the Russians do not view unfavorably. There is a mythology built around the wisdom of doing nothing. (Didn't Kutuzov defeat Napoleon by yielding, by giving that European invader enough Russian rope to hang himself?) At the same time, the Russians can be moved to accomplish heroic feats—fighting a Napoleon or a Hitler, or sending a man into space. But the day-to-day building of a sound and stable society has never been part of their experience. History has deprived them of the best and the worst of middle-class values. The U.S.S.R.'s democracy of poverty had satisfied the Russians. Now, desire and ambition are stimulated by the state, resulting in larger inequalities of wealth, a "culture of envy" as the journalist Hedrick Smith terms it. Not keeping up with the Ivanovs, tearing them down.

Soviet propaganda has been all too successful in equating business with greed, property with theft, profit with swindle. The Russians are aware of all their shortcomings in this regard and, as usual, shrug them off with a joke: The definition of Russian business—three guys steal a case of vodka, sell it for 200 rubles, and get drunk on the proceeds.

Now, as Russia has to leap through the void to its next historical incarnation, all the old questions return: Who really are the Russians? Whither Russia? What will happen? Scenarios and prescriptions abound, some wise, some foolish (though not impossible), and some even optimistic.

Writing well before the Gorbachev era, Poland's leading novelist, Tadeusz Konwicki, observed with prophetic irony, "We should thank God that Russia has been rendered inert by that idiotic doctrine of communism. Imagine a free, democratic Russia with a capitalist economy. In a few years a Russia of that sort would be producing art of such genius they'd have the world on its knees. A Russia like that would truly overtake America in industry."

A best-case scenario of the sort envisioned by Konwicki is not out of the question. As their history reveals, the Russians are amazingly hardy, vital, and resilient, with a marked preference for the dramatic. And what change could be more dramatic than Russia becoming democratic and capitalist? Nations can change. As another Pole remarked tartly to me when I questioned Poland's ability to create an orderly society, "But what about the Jews? Who would have ever suspected that the Jews, who cringed for 2,000 years, would suddenly become the best soldiers in the world once they had a country of their own?" Fair enough. And, unlike the Jews, the Russians don't have to travel thousands of miles to get a country of their own. It's right there beneath their feet. All they need is a sense that now at last their country belongs to them. But that will take time, and time, like everything else, is in short supply in Russia.

Values are also in short supply. In an essay published in an international edition of *Newsweek* in late 1990, Alexei Izyumov, a political analyst and economist at the Soviet Academy of Sciences, wrote, "Soviet society took only six years of *glasnost* to overcome most of the myths and fetishes of Communism that had been nurtured by the Soviet propaganda machine for nearly 70 years." But, he added, this is only the "first step of a badly needed ideological revolution; to complete it, the vacuum created in the minds of millions of Soviets by the swift demolition of old Communist gods has to be filled with a new set of heroes. And that seems a more difficult task."

But Izyumov's prescription is as weak as his analysis is strong. What's needed, he says, is a "massive educational campaign to fill the minds of disenchanted Soviets with the values and ideas that helped the nation of the civilized world to survive and prosper . . . the primacy of individual rights, respect for private ownership, the rule of law and ideological tolerance. . . . "

Izyumov is clearly a Westernizer of the Sakharov stripe. His calls for a "massive" campaign, however, betray a Soviet cast of mind, and his belief in the miraculous powers of education are all too reminiscent of previous generations of Russians dazzled by the light from the West. Values are not potatoes that can simply be shipped east, and tolerance is not a vaccine with which Soviet citizens can be inoculated.

Still, Izyumov is on target when he speaks of a void of values. And history abhors a vacuum every bit as much as nature does. The danger here is that fascism will fill the vacuum. The Russian fascists are still a fringe group, but the 20th century demonstrates that fringe groups can streak to power in times of crisis. After all, the Bolsheviks began as a marginal band of disgruntled intellectuals arguing about their arcane ideology. Today's ultra-nationalists appeal to Russian patriotism by calling for the restoration of what had been defiled under Communism—Russia's churches, Russia's rivers, Russia's soul. But they also appeal to Russian paranoia in seeking the "Enemy," the defiler of the motherland. Groups like Pamyat (meaning "memory" but implying vengeance) are clearly deranged in their belief that all Russia's sufferings were caused by a secret cabal of Jews and Freemasons. Still, they are symptomatic of the need to find some explanation for the trauma suffered by all Russia in the Soviet era. It could not all have been, as one banner proclaimed at a recent Moscow demonstration, 72 YEARS ON THE ROAD TO NOWHERE.

The Russian fascists offer the same thing fascists everywhere do—an answer, a scapegoat, a myth, a uniform, and the chance to do violence. Pamyat's official 60-point program of January 12, 1989, blueprints a future in which Russia is ruled by both the Church and the army, obsessed with the need to purge Russia of alien elements, to rid the economy of "Zionist capital," and to punish those responsible for the millions who died under Communism, which Pamyat calls "Zionist genocide." In this scenario, Russia ends the century with a bloodbath.

Some of the liberal intelligentsia favor a scenario that might be called the Chaadaev variation. Chaadaev was an early-19th-century Russian philosopher who was officially declared insane for daring to suggest that Russia belonged "to that number of nations which do not seem to make up an integral part of the human race, but which exist only to teach the world some great lesson." That lesson must be that the practice of Communism results in colossal tragedy. Having fulfilled its purpose, Russia loses its reason for being and simply fades away. I suppose it is conceivable that the Soviet Union could disintegrate without major violence. Worn out by suffering, exhausted by the costs of empire, Russia becomes just another country, a Czechoslovakia with 11 time zones. Its 1,000-year history ends with a whimper, not a bang. But the tens of thousands of nuclear missiles Russia now possesses make a bang more likely than a whimper.

Writer Alexander Solzhenitsyn (seen here in the gulag) argues for the formation of an all-Slavic federation and the introduction of democracy.

When Alexander Solzhenitsyn's essay "How to Revitalize Russia" was published in the U.S.S.R., it was read not once but twice by Mikhail Gorbachev. Solzhenitsyn's central thesis is that the burden of empire is killing Russia. Russia must give up the dream of empire and concentrate on healing its wounds and regaining its strength. The Baltic states, Armenia, Georgia, and the Asian republics should be allowed to secede freely, he argued. A new political entity would gradually come into being, an all-Slavic federation to be called the Russian Union and to consist of Russia proper, Belorussia, and the Ukraine. Democracy, which he now grudgingly accepts, should be introduced at the grass-roots level. The great Slavophile even called for that most Western of notions, free enterprise, but only as a concession to man's nature.

But Solzhenitsyn's plan would succeed only if the Ukrainians were to accept this vision of the Russians and Ukrainians as one people who "issued from the same city, Kiev," and were then separated only by the "tragedy of the Mongol Invasion" and the "dark years of Communism." Solzhenitsyn's solution embodies an unconscious imperialism to which the Ukrainians are sensitive. For centuries Russia has subjugated the Ukraine, scorning its culture as inferior. But Russia needs the food and energy of the Ukraine more than the Ukraine needs Russia. Had he suggested that the capital of the new Russia be Kiev, the city where its mutual history with the Ukraine began, his proposal might have sounded more inviting.

Gorbachev rejected Solzhenitsyn's ideas, though it has never been clear how Gorbachev saw the world, or what he ultimately stood for. Gorbachev's plan was to create a voluntary federation, retaining the name U.S.S.R., which would now signify the Union of Soviet *Sovereign* Republics instead of the Union of Soviet *Socialist* Republics. This was the sort of word magic, however, that no longer worked for miners who couldn't buy soap, or for mothers who had to get up at dawn to buy milk. In early 1991, after foreign minister Eduard Shevardnadze's dramatic resignation, Gorbachev seemed stranded in a lonely middle ground between those favoring faster change and those who thought too much had changed already, and for the worse. Russia's old tendency toward extremism was surfacing again. The very near future would show exactly how sincere were Gorbachev's intentions for reform. His crackdown on Lithuania, Latvia, and the press in early 1991 was either a classic case of two steps forward and one step back, or a case of two steps forward and two steps back. In any case, neither Mikhail the Reformer nor Mikhail the Restorer appeared to have much time.

Mikhail Gorbachev seemed stranded in the middle ground between those who favored change and those who thought too much had changed already.

Given the current circumstances in the Soviet Union, I cannot help but wonder what the worst-case scenarios for Russia might look like. Tragic finales are more typical of Russia than happy endings. The Russians themselves have a gloom-and-doom mentality: both at the kitchen table and in print, they indulge in apocalyptic prophecies.

Consider for a moment how the current situation could veer out of control. The economy continues to disintegrate; food is used as a political weapon. The result is large-scale starvation, no stranger to Russia. Western relief efforts bog down because of Soviet corruption and the woeful distribution system. Food riots erupt in major cities. Russia now splits into its two natural extremes: the Communists, who are fighting for their lives; and the Russian nationalists, who are fighting to be free of Communism. The KGB sides largely with the Communists. The army, remembering the injuries inflicted by Stalin in his purges and the strain on its honor caused by Afghanistan, goes over to the Russian nationalists. Mutinies spark armed engagements, which escalate into civil war.

Siberia breaks free of the U.S.S.R. and forms its own republic, heeding Solzhenitsyn's call for Russia to revitalize itself by shifting its center to the unspoiled lands of the Northeast. The Russian Republic is now broken into two parts, the Asian (Siberia) and European (as the territory west of the Urals is known). But then the central Communist government gives Siberia an ultimatum: renounce secession or Moscow will obliterate its new capital, Novosibirsk. The sailors in the U.S.S.R.'s nuclear submarine fleet, inspired by memories of the battleship *Potemkin* in the 1905 revolution and the 1921 Kronstadt uprising, threaten to retaliate with nuclear missiles if Novosibirsk is destroyed. The showdown has come.

Epic calamity is in the Russian blood. A hundred years ago, who could have imagined that tsardom would vanish, Communists would seize power, and 20 million lives would be lost in the 1918-20 civil war? Who could have foreseen that 23 million people would be killed under a Stalin—in the gulags, the execution cellars, and the starvation of the Ukraine? Who could have predicted that another 27 million Russian lives would be lost in World War II? And who could have conceived that in this century, Russia would experience three outbreaks of cannibalism—following the civil war, during collectivization (1930-32), and during the 900-day siege of Leningrad (1941-44)?

Thus I believe that Russia is unlikely to resolve its current crisis—to free itself from Stalin's system and the worst of its long past—without a great spasm of violence. What I foresee is a much scaled-down version of the worst-case scenario described above. A civil war is more than likely, but not one in which nuclear weapons are used. Nonetheless, conventional artillery shells could strike ill-housed reactors of the Chernobyl type, resulting in a series of nuclear incidents, just as Andrei Sakharov warned a few years ago.

No matter how I juggle the equation, it always comes out the same: Russia's history added to existing tensions plus thousands of nuclear weapons (and dozens of dangerous reactors) equals civil war, possibly with a nuclear dimension.

I hope I am wrong. I would much prefer to see Russians dancing in Red Square in gratitude to *their* grandfathers for remaining in their native land. Or, better still, not dancing, just going about their business with the dignity of citizens.

"We didn't just start an air express service. We started a revolution."

At Federal Express, we do a lot more than deliver packages and freight swiftly and dependably to more than 120 countries worldwide. We work in partnership with companies to design and operate the most sophisticated business logistics systems in the world. This allows companies to expand their markets, improve productivity, and compete more efficiently in a rapidly-changing global economy. You could call it revolutionary.

Additional Copies

To order additional copies of *Predicting Russia's Future* for friends or colleagues, please write to The Larger Agenda Series, Whittle Direct Books, 505 Market St., Knoxville, Tenn. 37902. For a single copy, please enclose a check for $11.95 payable to The Larger Agenda Series. When ordering 10 or more books, enclose $9.95 for each; for orders of 50 or more, enclose $7.95 for each. If you wish to order by phone, call 800-284-1956.

Also available, at the same prices, are copies of the previous books in The Larger Agenda Series: *The Trouble With Money* by William Greider, *Adhocracy: The Power to Change* by Robert H. Waterman Jr., *Life After Television* by George Gilder, *The Book Wars* by James Atlas, *The X Factor* by George Plimpton, *A Short History of Financial Euphoria* by John Kenneth Galbraith, and *Pacific Rift* by Michael Lewis.

Please allow two weeks for delivery.
Tennessee residents must add 7¾ percent sales tax.